The author

Alan Fowler has a career spanning the private and public sectors. He has held personnel appointments in the UK and overseas in four industries (engineering, shoe manufacture, sugar, construction) and in two of the largest local authorities. He is currently County Manpower Services Officer with Hampshire County Council, with a workforce of over 40,000 and 17 trade unions. In the 1970s he headed the Industrial Relations Division of the GLC, while in the private sector he had extensive negotiating experience at plant, company and industry levels.

He writes widely on personnel topics, is a member of the Editorial Board of the IPM's journal, *Personnel Management*, a Fellow of the IPM, an employer member of the industrial tribunals, and Manpower Correspondent for the *Local Government Chronicle*. His three latest books are *Personnel management in local government*, 2nd edition published in 1980 by the IPM, *Local authority manpower*, published in 1982 by BKT Publications, and *Getting off to a good start*, published by the IPM in 1983.

Effective Negotiation

Alan Fowler

Institute of Personnel Management

First published 1986

Phototypeset by Cotswold Typesetting Ltd
and printed in Great Britain by Dotesios Printers Ltd,
Bradford-on-Avon, Wiltshire

British Library Cataloguing Publication Data

Fowler, Alan
  Effective negotiation.
  1. Negotiation in business
  I. Title
  658.4'5   HD58.6

ISBN 0-85292-312-0

Contents

1 Negotiation: the basic principles

Everyone negotiates

Everyone negotiates. Two neighbours try to settle an argument as to how much each should pay towards the repair of a garden wall. A small boy suggests that if he is allowed to stay up late he will wash the car. A householder tries to get a reduction in the estimate for a plumbing repair by offering cash in advance. Three golf club committee members meet to settle their differences about the siting of a new tee.

In the business world, a marketing executive persuades a factory manager to alter a production schedule to fit in an order for a special customer. A sales representative tries to persuade a shop manager to display a particular brand more prominently.

Moving into a more formal arena, a quantity surveyor meets a building contractor to resolve claims made by the contractor for extra costs incurred by the client changing the specification while the work was in progress. A management team from an expanding retail chain bargains with the managers of a property company for special rental terms for being the first tenants of a new shopping precinct.

In Brussels, the European foreign ministers meet for a marathon negotiating session about farm prices; while in NATO, service chiefs haggle about the standardization of small arms ammunition.

In the more familiar world of personnel management, a shop steward sees her supervisor to try to obtain a withdrawal of disciplinary action against one of her members. In a London conference suite, the 40 or so members of the two sides of a national industrial joint council meet to hammer out a pay settlement.

In all these situations, despite massive differences of scale and subject matter, people are negotiating. Negotiation is not a specialist industrial relations function. Much of the decision-making process in the whole world of work is carried forward through formal and informal negotiation. Managers spend a large proportion of their time influencing and persuading other managers within their own organization over whom they have no executive authority. Analyses of managerial activity often show that managers spend only a minority of their time in contact with their subordinate staff – the staff they can direct on the basis of executive authority. A much larger proportion of their time is occupied in contacts with managerial colleagues in their own and other departments. In these lateral relationships, neither party has the authority to direct the other. If differences of interest, objective or opinion occur, matters are resolved by argument and persuasion, not by the issuing of orders. Arguing and persuading, influencing other people to move closer to one's own position, conceding changes in one's own stance, these are core activities in the wider process of negotiation.

Many managers also spend a great deal of time in contact with people outside their own organization – suppliers, customers, consultants, central and local government officers and many others. Again, in many of these contacts, differences have to be resolved by discussion. In the commercial and legal context, many of these transactions are recognized formally as negotiation. Those involved know that they are, as it were, wearing negotiating hats. They come to the negotiations with an expectation and understanding of a certain pattern of behaviour. The same managers, often confident and expert in this formal negotiating mode, may nevertheless be far less effective in informal, one-to-one discussions with managerial colleagues: or may feel ill at ease when faced across the negotiating table by an aggressive trade union official who does not share the same business values.

Yet there are many principles and skills common to all types of negotiation, and bargaining in an industrial relations context is not wholly different from the settlement, by discussion, of a supply contract or a legal dispute.

What is negotiation?

It is useful to start with some negatives. Negotiation does not occur where one party has the authority or the power unilaterally to impose a decision on the other. This is, perhaps, one reason why some managers find it difficult to come to terms with the process. If their perception of the ideal or model managerial role is authoritarian – the giving of instructions to subordinates or the exercise of superiority over competitors – then the acceptance that in many situations this simple concept will not bring results may be difficult. It is an underlying theme of this book that the occasions on which most managers can wield this simple authoritarian ability to impose their decisions are extremely limited. The achievement of most management objectives depends, if not on enthusiastic co-operation, then at least on action jointly agreed between individuals or organizations who do not initially perceive their interests as coincident.

Negotiation is not a single skill, or even group of skills. Skills are obviously involved, but negotiation in the broad sense used throughout this book is a process which takes place within particular contexts. The context, in terms of subject matter, the nature of the parties involved and the degree of formality, determines the particular skills needed in any specific negotiation situation. Some skills are common to all forms of negotiation. Some are specific to a particular context. The common elements are the basic characteristics of negotiation as a process. What are these elements?

- Negotiation involves two or more parties: no-one can negotiate in isolation.

- The parties must need each other's involvement in achieving some jointly desired outcome. The householder negotiating with the plumber needs a repair effected. The plumber needs the business. If either considers the other's position unacceptable, negotiation ceases because their common interest has disappeared.

- Although having this common interest, the parties start with different interests and objectives, and these differences prevent the achievement of an outcome. Negotiation is unnecessary if both parties agree without question not only on the outcome but also on the measures to achieve it. So negotiation is a process for the joint settlement of differences.

- The parties must, at least initially, consider negotiation to be a more satisfactory way of resolving their differences than alternative methods. If this view is not held, then no negotiation occurs and the

3

matter will be resolved by coercion, arbitration or by legal action. The fact that these alternatives are usually seen only as options when negotiations fail, indicates the strong, even if unconscious, view that negotiation is the most acceptable process for the resolution of differences.

- Each party must consider that there is some possibility of persuading the other to modify their initial position. There is no point in embarking on negotiations if one is convinced that the other party's position is wholly unchangeable. It might be thought that each party must also be prepared to accept compromise on their own position. It will be argued later that this is certainly desirable, but is not a wholly essential element when negotiating principles are being considered. Negotiations can certainly begin when one or even both parties have no intention of changing. The key point is that each retains some hope of their ability to persuade the other – even if their own determination to 'stick or bust' is ironclad.

- Similarly, each party must retain hope of an outcome which they can accept, and some concept of what this outcome might be. The outcome may not be particularly palatable, but it must at least be perceived to be acceptable – however reluctant this acceptance might be. Without this hope, and without such a concept, negotiation becomes meaningless.

- Each party must have some degree of power over the other's ability to act. The power may not be equal. The small boy who is bargaining about staying up late has far less power than his parents, who can bring the discussion to a close at any time by saying: 'Off to bed!' They might even risk forcing him to wash the car as well. But he is not wholly powerless. Even if a withdrawal of his offer to wash the car is ineffective, he can still exert influence by the unspoken knowledge of his parents that bad feelings might be created if they attempt too dictatorial and unsympathetic a conclusion. The potential to create a hassle, even when no other more powerful economic or legal weapons are available, is a potent underlying power issue in many negotiations, particularly those involving trade unions. If one party were entirely powerless, there would be no purpose in the other embarking on the negotiating process. Dictation would suffice.

● The negotiating process itself is essentially one of interaction between people – primarily direct verbal inter-communication, though in some cases with a significant written element. Even in the apparently most impersonal of written exchanges between, say, the boards of two companies, there is an essential, underlying, human or personal element. The words in impersonal and corporate documents have to be composed by people. The progress and outcome of negotiations are strongly influenced by human attitudes and emotions, not just by the logic of each party's arguments. Pride, anger, humour, fear, competitiveness – all are essential ingredients of the negotiation process.

When all these themes are put together, a definition of negotiation emerges which provides a useful summarized starting point for more detailed examination of the various parts of the process:

Negotiation is a process of interaction, by which two or more parties who need to be jointly involved in an outcome but who initially have different objectives, seek by the use of argument and persuasion, to resolve their differences in order to achieve a mutually acceptable solution. (Author's definition)

Differences in negotiation

So far, we have concentrated on principles which are common to all types of negotiation. It is equally important to identify the differences between various negotiating situations. The tactics and psychology of any actual negotiation are influenced significantly by the particularities of the situation, as well as by the underlying common principles.

● The definition above refers to two or more parties to negotiation. In practice, the number of parties is of great significance, as the difficulty of reaching a mutually agreed conclusion increases markedly with every addition to the number of those involved. The minimum, of course, is two, and many negotiators would argue that this is the ideal number. With just two parties it is relatively easy to keep track of the extent to which one, other or both are moving from their original positions towards a settlement. But involve a third party – let alone a fourth, fifth or sixth – and the course of interaction and compromise becomes very much more complex. It was a wise and essential principle of Whitleyism (the system of National Joint Councils introduced into industry and the public sector after the First World War) to require national multi-union and multi-employer negotiating bodies to form two sides, each of which resolved any internal differences before meeting each other.

● The quality or style of negotiating is also influenced by the number of participants on each side. The simplest, though not necessarily the easiest, negotiating situation is between two individuals. In practice, a single party to a negotiation can consist of any number of negotiators from one, when buyer meets seller or supervisor meets shop steward, to upwards of 100 in, for example, the trade union side of a major multi-union national negotiating committee. Obviously it is quite impossible for such a large number of individuals all to participate in the to and fro of a negotiating discussion. Between one and five active participants on each side probably represents the upper and lower limits of effective negotiation, and in a later chapter, the mechanics of negotiating with much larger sides are examined in detail.

● Negotiations have a different quality depending on whether those involved are negotiating on their own behalf, or are acting as representatives. The householder negotiating with the plumber is not accountable to anyone else. He or she can set their own limits and objectives, and make instant decisions. The personnel manager, negotiating for the company and the full-time trade union official negotiating for the membership at large, are less free. Their role is that of representatives of wider interests from whence they derive their authority to act, and which may impose limits on the extent to which they may offer compromise solutions and conclude eventual agreements. There are advantages and disadvantages to both the direct and representative roles. The former permits of more rapid and resolute decisions, but is an exposed position with no fall-back facility. The latter, if negotiating authority is too limited, may undermine the credibility of the negotiator, but it does provide opportunities for gaining time by referring back (or up) for new directions, and offers the possibility of breaking a deadlock by moving the negotiations up to a new, higher arena.

- There may be wide differences of power or influence between the parties to a negotiation. Their relative strength is rarely in total balance, and the realities of this distribution of power between them will influence the outcome. On a theoretical and logical basis, if one party is perceived as controlling 75 per cent of the situation and the other 25 per cent, then the likely eventual compromise between their two differing opening positions is not the classic 50/50 ('split the difference'), but a solution in which the weaker party has had to move 75 per cent of the way towards the stronger. In reality, it is rarely possible to assess relative strength so precisely, and in any event the outcome of negotiation will be influenced by other factors, such as the skill and persistence of the participants and their own perceptions of each other's strengths.

  Assessments of strength, and of the power of each party to coerce or pressurize the other, are nevertheless of major importance to the effective conduct of a negotiation.

- There are, also, two major and different types of power or influence. One is specific to the issue being negotiated: the other is more general.

  Thus, in a commercial negotiation about, say, office rentals, the ultimate power each party has is to break off negotiations, part company entirely, and seek a different client or property owner. In a legal negotiation about a financial settlement, power will be influenced by one party's ability to pay and the extent of the other's financial need. In these examples, power and influence is limited to the matter under negotiation.

  In trade union negotiations, however, each party's power extends much beyond whatever topic is being discussed. Thus, although the negotiations may be about the dismissal of a single employee, the trade union may threaten the use of its very much wider power to call all the employees out on strike. In another negotiation, limited in specific subject matter to, say, a productivity scheme, the employer's ultimate power may extend much more

7

widely to shutting a factory or to the withdrawal of the trade union's facility to receive dues through a check-off system.

How widely power and influence are available is an important feature for negotiators to assess.

● There is a related factor. This is the nature of the relationship between the parties, whether this extends beyond the confines of the particular negotiation, and if so, to what extent.

For the quantity surveyor who is negotiating a builder's claims, the relationship between his company and the builder is probably limited to that one negotiation. In consequence, the negotiating process will not be influenced by any other factors than those specific to the financial point at issue.

At the other extreme, the small boy's discussion with his parents, the supervisor's argument with the shop steward, and a company's annual wage negotiation with its trade unions, all take place within the context of a long-term or permanent relationship between the two parties. Their conduct of negotiations about any individual issue will inevitably be influenced by their perceptions as to the effect the quality and outcome of the negotiations will have on this more general relationship. An abrasive style of negotiating which might get satisfactory results in a single transaction untramelled by any worry about after-effects, might well be disastrous in a different situation in which it did serious damage to long-term relationships.

● Negotiations range from the very informal to the highly formal and structured. Formal negotiations, such as national annual pay bargaining for an entire industry, take place within a known and prescribed framework of structure and procedure. Each side may have the services of a full-time secretariat. The negotiations will probably follow an established procedure, beginning with the tabling of an extensively documented claim, followed by a written employers' response and then a lengthy process of debate on offers, counter claims and revised offers. The negotiations will conclude with the almost ritual signing of an agreement.

At the other extreme, informal transactions may not even be recognized as negotiation. As an example, consider a housing manager of a local authority who approaches the Borough treasurer trying to persuade him to ease a revenue budgeting problem by reclassifying a large item of maintenance expenditure from revenue to capital. She may not consider her approach as one of negotiation, but merely as an informal attempt to persuade a colleague to be helpful. Yet this transaction may well display all the elements of negotiation.

The advantages of formal negotiating are that no time or energy is wasted discussing procedures or roles. These are all established by the formal system and structure. Similarly, the subject matter of the negotiation is clearly defined, making it easier for the participants to resist being diverted into arguments about unrelated or peripheral issues. Against these advantages, and in favour of the informal mode, the formal approach restricts both the range of discussion and its conduct. Potential deadlock may be avoided in informal negotiations because there are no rules against deferral of discussions, changing the subject, or changing the participants. These tactics are not so readily available in the less flexible arena of the highly formal bargaining session.

2 Stages in the negotiating process

The negotiating process is not a single activity. It proceeds over a period of time and the strategies and skills appropriate to one phase are not suitable in others. Designers of training courses in negotiation usually stress the importance of thinking of negotiation as a series of stages. While differing in detail, all recognize three main stages:

1   What happens .before negotiations begin: the background, or sequence of events, which lead to negotiation occurring.

2   What happens in the course of the actual negotiation – which may in turn be broken down into several stages.

3   What happens when the negotiations are concluded: the extent to which the agreement reached has its desired effect and is effectively implemented.

As with the general principles discussed in the preceding chapter, these three stages are applicable to all types of negotiation, formal or informal, and are not limited to the industrial relations scene. They are, though, of particular relevance to negotiations in which the two parties, as with employers and trade unions, have a long-term or permanent working relationship outside the narrow confines of the conference room.

Each of these three stages needs to be considered in some detail.

Before negotiation occurs

The quality and success (or failure) of any particular negotiation is strongly influenced by the nature of the events which lead to negotiation being necessary. In some cases negotiation is a normal and necessary part of a wider transaction. For example, the retail company which is planning to open a store in a new shopping precinct knows from the beginning that there will come a stage in this project when formal negotiations will be necessary with the property company about rentals. The key to these negotiations being effective will lie very much with planning and preparation. Accurate cost and profit projections will determine the upper limit of an acceptable rental. Commercial intelligence about the demand for shop space will help in assessing the strength of an argument for special terms. A knowledge of the going rate for rentals in other shopping developments may help to counter some of the property company's proposals. Neither party will consider the negotiations to be other than an ordinary business transaction.

In an industrial relations dispute, the position may seem to be very different, at least to the management. The firm and its managers will see their primary and normal role to be the pursuit of the company's business objectives, in this case, perhaps, the opening of a Saturday shift to speed completion of an important contract. The trade union's objection unless a contract completion bonus is paid, and the consequent negotiations, will probably be seen as an unexpected and frustrating interruption to normality. The trade union, of course, will consider its action as a necessary measure to meet the union's primary objective – protecting and improving the rights and benefits of its members. So the trade union officials will probably go into negotiation well prepared, and certainly with the attitude that negotiating is their normal business. To start negotiations with one party confident in their role and possibly looking forward to the bargaining session with some relish, while the other party is resentful about having to spend time on what is seen as an unjustifiable interruption to other more important matters, will not augur well for the latter's success.

Preparation for effective negotiation therefore consists of more than researching the background, and planning specific bargaining ploys. It includes an attitudinal element – ensuring that potential progress is not prejudiced by carrying resentment or other negative feelings into the bargaining session.

It also has to be recognized that the highly structured or detailed type of preparation for negotiation often propounded by trainers cannot be applied directly to many of the informal transactions which occur, for example when a shop steward appears suddenly in a supervisor's office, raising as a matter of urgency, a wholly unforeseen and unexpected problem. Even in these circumstances, however, the basic principles of the pre-negotiation stage apply. They may be considered as a series of questions.

What kinds of issues are likely to arise within the general work context which may require negotiation?

This is a very general point about awareness. Managers should be aware of the whole range of relationships and contacts involved in their work, and of the subjects or situations in these relationships which are likely to need negotiation. So it should not be a surprise to the production manager if the finance director questions a sudden change in the production department's method of cost control. The production manager should know, and attitudinally accept, that the finance director 'owns' the subject of cost accounting procedures, and that if Production want to change them, the changes will need negotiation with Finance. On the industrial relations front, it should similarly not be a matter of surprise or resentment that shop stewards will question, and probably oppose, any unilaterally imposed changes in shift schedules, safety regulations, payment systems or disciplinary procedures.

A state of understanding and general readiness about who owns or claims a right of involvement in particular topics or decisions will go a long way towards meeting the need for preparation for negotiation which may, on the face of it, seem difficult to achieve in the informal setting.

What is the real issue?

A disagreement or dispute occurs, and negotiations seem likely. Before going ahead, it is important to check that the issue raised is the real problem.

It is far from unusual for trade union officials (and individual employees) to raise one issue when the real concern is with a related, but less obvious matter. So a personnel manager may receive a claim from the shop steward of a particular section that the heating should be improved. That matter is dealt with – only to be followed by a complaint about high noise levels. Both complaints may be little more than symptoms of a deeper problem, perhaps that personal relationships between the steward and the section manager have deteriorated. The perceptive personnel manager will talk the whole situation through with the steward to discover the real issues before arguing about the temperature or noise.

Who is involved?

Even in the most informal and unexpected of negotiations, a quick mental check as to who needs to be involved in the issue is essential. 'Why wasn't I asked?' is a common complaint when a negotiating transaction has been concluded to the satisfaction of the two parties initially involved, by someone who also has an interest in the outcome but was left out of the discussion. Important agreements can fall apart when this happens. Consider, for example, the quick deal done with a manual trade union about, say, Saturday shift working, which fails to take account of the need on this shift for the attendance of a few non-manual employees, members of a white collar union. It may well be that these staff are themselves quite happy about the arrangement. Their union, however, may well make a blocking objection, not because of the issue itself, but because they have taken offence, on principle, to being overlooked in the negotiating process.

This is a danger not always recognized by individual managers in their dealings with each other. In a sugar refinery, the chief chemist and chief engineer negotiated a slight modification to a routine maintenance schedule to their mutual advantage, but neither stopped to consider whether any other interest was involved. There was such an interest – the stores manager – as the change required the fitters to draw some stores materials during the night shift from a section of the stores which was previously shut down at the end of the day shift. Again, resentment at being overlooked or taken for granted, rather than the issue itself, caused the biggest problem in achieving an eventual solution.

Is negotiation necessary?

Not every issue which is raised as a negotiating item need necessarily be resolved in that way. Negotiating is often a lengthy process. There may be a quicker solution.

So two managers who come into dispute, both realizing that neither has the power to achieve a satisfactory solution, may opt to save time and energy and refer the matter directly to the chief executive for a ruling. In effect, this is the use of arbitration instead of, not after, abortive negotiation.

Shop stewards will often treat an issue as negotiable when in fact the management has the authority and power to decide it unilaterally. Negotiation should not be conceded merely because it is sought. This is a lesson frequently demonstrated in the commercial world when a buyer without real purchasing clout attempts to negotiate price reductions from a major supplier. He is likely to be told: 'Buy at our price or not at all. Our quoted prices are non-negotiable.'

Not that the avoidance of negotiation need always be confrontational. The discussion with the shop steward who is complaining about inadequate heating may be turned by the personnel manager from a negotiating to a counselling session. Drawing out the real issue – poor staff/manager relations – and advising the shop steward how to proceed, may be far more effective and less abrasive than an argument about temperatures.

Finally, there is always the possibility that the right response to a claim is to concede it without argument. Just because a trade union asks for something is not of itself sufficient reason to seek an alternative solution. It may be that the request or claim is reasonable. If so, the quicker and more readily it is conceded, the better. Unnecessary negotiation, followed by what might be perceived as grudging acceptance of the union's position, will lose all the advantage to be gained by the possibly unexpected or unconventional immediate 'yes'.

What is the quality of the relationship between the parties?

Before plunging into negotiation, it is usually worth considering the importance (if any) of the general quality of the working relationship between the parties, and of the impending negotiations on this relationship. In short-term commercial situations, the issue is unimportant or irrelevant. The relationship is limited to the particular transaction. But there are many other situations in which the parties have a long-term relationship. Here, poor or good relations preceding the negotiation will have a significant impact on how constructively the negotiations proceed. Similarly, the quality of personal interaction within the negotiation – and its outcome – will affect future working relationships. This should not be taken as implying that the right stance in all negotiations is affable, relaxed and conciliatory on the grounds that this will assist future relationships. It may be that past relationships have become too comfortable, with the management conceding trade union claims too readily, and the trade union assuming it has only to bluster to achieve what it wants. If this is the analysis, then perhaps the forthcoming negotiation is the opportunity to achieve a necessary change.

The important point is the analysis: knowing about the relationship, thinking through its impact on the negotiations and on how the negotiation will affect working contacts in future.

During negotiation

This major phase in the whole process is dealt with in detail in subsequent chapters. Here, it is sufficient to note that the apparently simple activity of a group of people sitting at a table and arguing their initial differences through to an eventual agreement has many dimensions. There are many different negotiating systems, even within the single field of industrial relations. There is a whole range of tactics and ploys. Effective negotiation also utilizes a number of different skills. All these topics are covered in Chapters 4–8.

Before going into this detail it is helpful to consider the main stages of the negotiation itself:

Defining the issue: good negotiators check with each other, before getting involved in detailed argument, that there is at least a common understanding of what it is that they differ about.

Defining initial positions: each side sets out what it is seeking, or if the negotiation is on a claim by one side only, then that side puts and explains its claim and the other side gives an initial response.

The argument: a less definitive stage in which the initial positions are challenged and tested in argument.

Exploring possibilities: emerging from the argument, the two sides may begin to float new ideas to see what response occurs. These ideas may emerge almost imperceptibly at this stage and are not firm proposals.

Defining proposals: arising from the speculative possibilities just floated, firm propositions begin to emerge. If more than one simple issue is under debate, permutations of proposals in various 'packages' may be put forward. These may require a second stage of argument and exploration: indeed, this process may be repeated many times as proposals are made, responded to, amended, re-tabled, argued and modified.

Defining and concluding the agreement: eventually a proposal, or package of proposals, begins to emerge as a probable satisfactory outcome. Identifying the point at which it is safe to stop bargaining and propose a final solution may not be easy. Tried too soon, it may lose an agreement. Left too late, the other party may think of new angles. It is also important in concluding the negotiations to ensure that all parties have a common, unambiguous understanding of what they are about to agree. One of the most discouraging experiences for a negotiator is to conclude an exhausting negotiation apparently satisfactorily, only to have the whole thing fall apart the following day because the other party misunderstood the agreement.

After the negotiation

Concluding an agreement is not an end in itself. The purpose of any agreement is to produce a particular outcome. Of course, in many relatively simple negotiations, an agreement is coincident with the outcome. The tourist bargaining in a North African market agrees a price, pays, and gets the goat-skin slippers. But at the other extreme, a company which negotiates a flexible working agreement with three craft unions is by no means home and dry. As much, or more, effort may be needed to ensure implementation as went into the negotiation.

Several practical steps can be suggested:

1   *Include an implementation programme in the agreement.* Agreements often require action by both parties to achieve full implementation. It may be helpful, therefore, to set out in the agreement not just what is to be done, but who is to do what, and in what time scales. So the flexible working agreement will say that specific stages are to be reached in particular departments or workshops by specified dates, and will define which managers and which shop

stewards will take responsibility for informing particular groups of employees, and for monitoring progress.

2   *Set up a joint implementation review team.* To secure the continued commitment of both parties to the agreement's full implementation it may be useful for the negotiating teams to nominate a small joint review team to whom reports are given of progress, and which has authority to negotiate on minor, unforeseen difficulties which impede progress. Of course, if a major snag arises, it may be necessary to reconvene the full negotiating group.

3   *Ensure adequate information and explanation.* Many major industrial relations agreements depend for their success on the actions of literally thousands of managers and employees. Even in a small company, a deal struck between the managing director and the local trade union organizer needs to be communicated effectively to supervisors and staff.

Too often, this communication is limited to the posting of a few incomprehensible notices, and a relaying of information from top management to first-line supervisors by unreliable word-of-mouth messages which become increasingly distorted as they go down the management chain. Too often, also, this information is limited to a stark description of the details of the agreement, without explanation of the broader purpose or strategy which led to the particular form the agreement is in. Informing the employees may also be left entirely to the trade union officials.

Any agreement of any substance or complexity merits a carefully designed and efficiently executed programme of information and explanation. It is particularly important, in an industrial relations setting, that informing the workforce is not left solely to the trade unions. They will no doubt take steps to publicize the agreement to their members, but they will often put a particular gloss on the agreement, designed to highlight the advantages to their side and show their negotiators in a good light.

The most credible form of information is, of course, a joint one, as neither party can then be accused of distorting the agreement to enhance its own position. Meetings of workpeople, addressed jointly by managers and trade union officials, will go a long way to preventing such difficulties. Where this is not practicable, it is still important for management to get its message directly to the employees, and not leave this to the trade unions. Notices are probably one of the least effective methods. Other important channels of information are:

Briefing groups in which each manager and supervisor explains the agreement to their own small groups of staff. This obviously requires accurate and thorough pre-briefing of managers.

Letters, direct to employees' homes.

Video presentations – particularly useful to explain such things as an impending move to a new factory.

Company news sheets.

Each situation has to be assessed separately, as the right forms of communication in one instance may not suit another. The important point is always to ask: 'Who needs to know about and understand this agreement? How is ·this communication best effected? By whom? ·Within what time-scales?'

3 The industrial relations setting

Although the nature and style of negotiations in the context of industrial relations vary considerably from case to case, there are some general characteristics which influence all such transactions between employers and trade unions. The two most important of these influences are, firstly, the wider and longer term relationships within which negotiation occurs; secondly, the expectations which managers, trade union officials and shop stewards have about the accepted modes of behaviour and procedure applying to the negotiating process.

Thomason[1] points out that 'a negotiation may be conceived as an episode in a set of continuing relationships, so that the episode may reflect a history and will look forward to some future'. In other words, any negotiation will be affected by the quality of the relationships which the two parties have already established, and by their views as to how the negotiation will affect this relationship in future.

Kniveton and Towers,[2] with other commentators on collective bargaining, point to the importance of 'ritual' in determining how the parties to a negotiation will behave. By ritual, they mean 'the procedural steps which all parties feel obliged to carry out even though they are fully aware that to all intents and purposes it is for show'. As an example they quote the practice of a trade union in pitching its initial claim at a higher level than it expects eventually to settle for, and the conventional employers' response of a lower offer than the union is expected to accept. In that both parties are fully aware of these respective ploys, the two approaches negate each other and have little logical value. The routine of high claim, low offer, seems necessary not so much as an essential method of identifying a solution, but more as ritualistic behaviour which provides a degree of security or certainty in an otherwise uncomfortably unpredictable situation. Certainly, keeping to the generally accepted rules of the negotiating game seems to be important to managers and trade unionists provided one or both are seeking to avoid direct confrontation. Breaking these negotiating conventions, for example by one side issuing an inflammatory press statement while negotiations are still in progress, is a sure way of creating a situation which will be difficult to resolve by normal negotiating processes.

Although these general influences can be summarized in these two ways – the total relationship and ritual – it is helpful to examine what Thomason calls 'the conventions of negotiation' in more detail. He identifies the following six main factors:

- The quality of personal relationships
- Formal procedures
- The importance of precedents
- The process of making concessions
- Sanctions and pressures
- Maintaining integrity and good faith.

Personal relationships

The effective conduct of negotiations is markedly assisted if the participants understand and, if not like, at least respect, each other. Similarly, personal animosity or distrust creates a major barrier to the joint exploration of possible compromise which lies at the heart of the negotiation process. One feature of the miners' dispute of 1984/85 was the obvious and intense personal feelings displayed publicly towards each other by Messrs Scargill and Macgregor. It was difficult to see how effective negotiations could proceed between these two participants while each was being so openly dismissive of the other's credibility. Any manager or shop steward who has an interest in the prevention of disputes, or if they occur, in their rapid resolution, needs to consider very carefully how to establish and maintain constructive working relationships with those with whom they may from time to time have to negotiate.

This is not a matter of trying to develop personal friendships. What is needed is a sound, personal but *working* relationship. It does not imply the adoption of false *bonhomie*. Indeed, any form of artificiality or patronizing behaviour will undermine the type of relationship which is needed. Much of the power and influence of a manager or trade union official is based on information – knowing what is happening within the organization, having advance knowledge of new developments, knowing about the moods and attitudes of managers and workpeople. Experienced and able industrial relations practitioners on the management and trade union sides trade in such information for their mutual benefit. Each knows that there are limits to what the other can reveal, but by maintaining frequent, highly informal and conversational contact, each is able from time to time to put the other in an advantageous position by revealing a useful piece of information, on the unspoken understanding that the other will in due course reciprocate. So a personnel manager, happening to run across the factory convenor in the canteen, might say: 'I don't know whether you've heard yet, George, but we might need to come to you formally fairly soon to discuss an increase in stock losses from the stores. It's a bit worrying because the security people tell us they can't rule out pilfering. You might find it helpful to do a bit of scouting round yourself informally before we raise it at the next meeting with the stewards.'

Clearly, the personnel manager is taking a risk in saying this. The convenor might react by formally objecting to the implication that some of his members are stealing. More seriously, the convenor might tip off all concerned and thus prejudice the company's security investigations. But if the manager and the convenor understand each other, the benefits will justify the risk. Quite apart from the actual question of the stock losses is the unspoken implication, or informal bargain, that this type of confidence from the personnel manager to the convenor will in due course be reciprocated. In other words, what is being established is almost a trading relationship. So the time will come, a week or so after the canteen conversation, when the convenor will drop into an apparently casual chat with the personnel manager a comment that: 'By the way, Fred the Red will be up for election as tool-room steward next month. He stands a pretty good chance if the tool-room manager persists with his daft plan for publicizing individual quality records.' Just factory gossip? Very much not. This piece of information is not just part of the trade-off of items of possible interest. The convenor knows that the personnel manager is not too happy about the tool-room manager's plans for quality records. So what the personnel manager is being given is some useful ammunition for this battle, the outcome of which will suit the convenor, who is therefore prepared to exploit the management's dislike of a potential shop steward, even to the latter's disadvantage. For both the personnel manager and the convenor, this wholly informal transaction is perceived as preferable to dealing with differences of view about quality records through the process of formal negotiation. On a more general basis, this type of interchange of information creates a depth of understanding, mutual obligation and 'feel' for the management and trade union viewpoints which will be of considerable assistance to both sides in achieving effective negotiations when a negotiating episode eventually becomes necessary on whatever topic.

Formal procedures

It would be wrong to give the impression that the quality of negotiations is influenced solely by the type of informal contact and relationship just described. These personal and informal factors are important, but the way in which most negotiations proceed is also determined by the existence of formal procedure agreements and conventions. There are two main aspects to this.

Firstly, there are disputes agreements which, *inter alia*, set out how negotiations are to be initiated, within what time-scales, and who participates in which form or level of negotiating meeting. The purpose of a disputes procedural agreement is wider than just the setting out of these negotiating drills. But the drills are necessary to ensure that no avoidable problems or delays occur. Without a procedure having been established, the settlement of a dispute about, say, overtime premia could well be prejudiced by a lengthy preliminary wrangle about how the negotiations are to be set up. Thus if the issue is seen by the trade union as domestic to one department they may object to the involvement of a headquarters personnel manager. Conversely, if the management see the matter simply as a little local difficulty, they might object to the presence at the negotiating table of a full-time regional trade union official. The purpose of procedural agreements is to set up agreed drills which enable both parties to concentrate on the real issues, rather than on the mechanics of the negotiating process. The three main elements in such agreements are usually:

1   *Time-scales:* ie meetings to be held within a specified number of working days of the dispute occurring.

2   *Levels:* specifying which issues are to be negotiated at which levels in the organization's hierarchy. Thus in a large local authority, three negotiating levels might be established at workplace, departmental and Council levels.

3   *Participants:* setting out who takes part on each side at each level. In the local authority example this might be workplace stewards and supervisors at level 1; departmental union representatives and departmental managers at level 2; and union branch executive members and elected councillors at level 3, each side assisted at this top level by professional advisers – the personnel manager advising the councillors and a full-time regional official advising the trade union side. The agreement may also specify the permitted numbers on each side; a useful safeguard against, for example, the whole shop stewards' committee turning up to pressurize a solo manager.

The second main, formal influence on the conduct of negotiations may not be wholly documented. It is the way in which each side actually conducts the presentation and discussion of its case. Some aspects of this may be prescribed. It is quite common, for example, for procedure agreements which apply at company or industry level to specify that if either party wishes a matter to be discussed, then a written notification must be made to the other party at least so many days before the meeting, and that this must be followed by the submission of a written case statement. It is also normal for agreements to state how the negotiating meetings are to be chaired. But there will also be a number of unwritten conventions, established by custom and practice. These are likely to include:

1   *Spokespersons:* that is, the nomination by each side of a principal speaker – particularly when, as in national negotiations, there are a large number of representatives on each side.

2   *Conduct of the meeting:* the ritual process of opening statements by each side's spokesperson, possibly followed by an adjournment, then follow-up statements leading on to more of a free-for-all in which the principal speakers will play a much less prominent part, then a further adjournment followed by a formal offer from the employers' spokesperson . . . and so on.

3   *Minutes:* the written agreement may specify how minutes are to be produced, agreed and published, but this is often left to custom and practice, and commonly to the management side. Although having this control over the documented record of the negotiations has its advantages, it is also part of the unwritten rules of the game that management will not exploit this potential benefit by distorting the record in the employers' favour. Indeed, any obvious attempt to do so will probably result in a demand by the trade union side for a formally prescribed method in which they see and agree the minutes in draft before issue.

4   *Announcements about agreements:* there will usually be an established procedure for the announcement of the details of agreements once these have been concluded. Sometimes this is by separate notices produced by each side. More effective, particularly in the sense of aiding implementation, is the issue of the agreement with an explanatory note co-signed by the employers' and trade unions' spokespersons.

Precedents

Custom and practice regarding the conduct of negotiations is only one aspect of the powerful influence which precedent has in the field of industrial relations. Precedents will also be quoted by both parties in support of their respective negotiating positions. Formally, previous agreements on whatever topics will be treated as binding (in honour, not in law) until they are superseded by new agreements. This has the advantage of providing for stability in relations between the parties, but can also create major problems when one party considers an old agreement to have become outdated and unacceptable, but the other party takes the view that the agreement is still satisfactory and is therefore unwilling to renegotiate the issue.

Less formally, both parties are likely to refer back to established practices and previous decisions, documented or not, as creating a pattern of rights. Thus the trade union may object to a dismissal for taking scrap material home without permission on the grounds that this practice has been going on for years and no-one has ever been dismissed for it before. The management may try to counter this argument by producing details of two earlier resignations which, they say, occurred only because the employees concerned realized they had been seen taking scrap and jumped the gun on dismissal by immediate resignations. It is noteworthy that arguments of this kind about past history often absorb as much negotiating time as any discussion about the specifics of the particular case. The standard trade union position is that if something has been done in a particular way in the past, then any change in this practice must be subject to negotiation. The management position is often that provided *some* evidence can be produced to show that the change is not entirely without precedent, then no negotiation is necessary. Either way, the existence or absence of precedent seems to be accepted by managers and trade unionists as a powerful argument for or against any particular view.

Concessions

Thomason refers to 'the notion of fairness in negotiation, for example, that it is only fair that each side should make approximately equal sacrifices in order to obtain agreement'. The importance of equal movement by each side may be overstated as either party which feels itself to be in a relatively weak position may well be satisfied with almost any movement by its more powerful opponent. But the main point remains, that both parties accept that the essence of negotiation is some willingness to depart from the original positions. In other words, both parties understand that a large element of negotiation is the making of concessions. Each expects this of the other. Each (normally) has some willingness itself to concede changes to its opening stance.

Obviously, negotiation is impossible if both parties, starting with different views, adamantly refuse to concede any change. Occasionally, though, one party will consider that it is possible for it to hold to its original position and to persuade the other to make all the concessions. Such tactics are very rarely successful at the negotiating table, though they may be achieved by using more coercive means. Fords on one occasion opened their annual pay bargaining with a first and final offer. It did not stick. The trade unions were able to insist on 'real' negotiations, and once these were conceded it became impossible for the company to hold rigidly to its first offer. There have been similar cases in which trade unions have attempted to stick to their original pay claims, but have eventually found it necessary to make concessions by lowering their sights after being lured into negotiation. The very process or experience of negotiation carries its own compulsion to compromise, and compromise means concession.

Sanctions and pressures

Although in some senses negotiation is an alternative to more direct forms of persuasive or coercive action, it is part of the accepted mythology or ritual of negotiation that some forms of sanction or pressure are still permissible. Thomason suggests, for example, that for a trade union to call an overtime ban to 'support' negotiations may be tolerated, but the calling of a strike while negotiations are still in progress would probably shift the dispute into a different arena. It is certainly a common employers' view that negotiations should not take place under this degree of duress. Similarly, a management's sudden dismissal of employees supporting an overtime ban while negotiations are taking place would be seen by the trade union as going too far in the use of sanctions, and would probably lead to negotiations being broken off. On the other hand, the union might, however reluctantly, tolerate the management's suspension of an attendance bonus during a bout of 'withdrawal of normal co-operation' without bringing active negotiations to a halt.

No definitive and generally applicable guidelines can be given because this factor is heavily dependent on the very different concepts of what is or is not acceptable in different organizations and industries. Some have abandoned the old convention of not negotiating under duress, and conduct negotiations while strikes are in progress almost as a matter of course. Others may see any form of sanction as unacceptable all the while negotiations still hold some likelihood of success.

One fairly recent development by trade unions and employers is the use of the media to explain their respective positions in an attempt to influence both public and employees and thereby the outcome of the negotiations. Although this is a discernible trend, the absence as yet of any very clear-cut practice and precedent makes its impact and acceptability unpredictable. Some trade unions will object strongly to management issuing any form of press release, let alone purchasing advertising space to get their message across. Other trade unions already make extensive use of local press and radio regardless of most employers' dislike for conducting negotiations through the media. Given the general growth of awareness about the value of public opinion, the importance of open information, and the impact of good presentation, it seems probable, however, that this use of the media will become an established and accepted form of influencing negotiations. From an employer's viewpoint, perhaps the most important single rule in using the media in this way is to ensure the total accuracy of whatever statements are issued or published. It is all too easy to acquire an adverse reputation as an untrustworthy employer by rushing into public print with distorted or incorrect statements for which embarrassing corrections or apologies have later to be issued.

Integrity

Effective negotiations, and this implies the conclusion of agreements which can successfully be implemented, require each party to have confidence in the good faith of the other. This factor is strongly influenced by the first of the six characteristics discussed in this chapter – the quality of the personal relationships which those involved in the negotiations have established outside the negotiating context. Integrity is also necessary within the negotiations. There are several aspects to this.

First, while it is accepted behaviour during a bargaining session to be selective in the use of facts, to exaggerate, to claim importance for minor matters, and to use threats as well as inducements, it is unacceptable and damaging actually to lie. Effective negotiation becomes impossible if the parties detect downright dishonesty and deceit.

Secondly, there are times when it may be helpful to either party to make statements in confidence, or to put forward propositions without commitment. Provided the party concerned makes clear the confidential or provisional nature of such statements, it is essential that the other party respects such limitations. To publicize as an offer an idea which has been put purely hypothetically in order to explore possibilities, is one way of destroying the trust which each side must have in the other's integrity if negotiations are ever to get past the first ritualistic or formal statements of opposing positions.

Finally, if threats, warnings or promises are made, it is best that they be real and kept. British Leyland in the pre-Edwardes era too often gave warning of the dire consequences of union action, only to fail to carry out the threat when the unions called the employer's bluff. Both sides had to go through some very painful experiences before the unions (and, perhaps some managers) realized that when Sir Michael Edwardes said that a factory would be closed if agreement could not be reached about wages and manning levels, he meant it.[3] This is a feature of industrial relations negotiations which is not limited to the employers. Trade unions, at individual shop steward level as well as in national negotiations, often damage their credibility by uttering dire but unfounded warnings about the probability of strike action. Once management gain the impression that such warnings are merely hollow rhetoric, they not only lose any impact, they also undermine the ability of the union to convince the management of the integrity of its whole position.

Other factors

In addition to Thomason's six points described earlier, there are two other factors in the industrial relations context which have a major influence on the nature and style of individual negotiations. These are:

- The type of negotiating session and its degree of formality

- The roles of the participants as lay representatives or professionals.

Negotiating sessions vary from the very informal to the highly formal and structured. At the most informal end of the spectrum is the meeting between an individual supervisor and an individual shop steward. As has been pointed out in the previous chapter, it may not be clear whether such a meeting really constitutes a negotiation. It may start as a conversation, or the interchange of information, and drift into counselling, consultation or bargaining. It is important, however, to recognize when the bargaining or negotiation phase occurs. Managers are sometimes caught out by having a shop steward claim that they have agreed something – implying a formal bargain – when the manager thought all that was happening was an informal, off-the-record exchange of possible ideas. Effective managers will spot the point at which wily stewards are trying to lure them into making firm commitments in the course of apparently informal conversation, and will say: 'That's something we will need to talk about more formally.' Or perhaps: 'That's something I need time to think about; come and see me about it tomorrow.'

At the other end of the spectrum is the big, set-piece national pay negotiation. This will be subject to defined and structured negotiating procedures in which the element of ritual will be far more dominant than in the one-to-one manager/shop steward contacts. A major feature of this type of negotiation is that each side fields a large negotiating team. In many cases, the team members are representatives of a number of different employer's and trade unions. In local government, for example, the employer's side of the National Joint Council for Manual Workers consists of 41 representatives drawn from some 450 local councils; the trade union side is a team of 26 representatives from four trade unions. Not only is it necessary for negotiations to be conducted by a very much smaller group of spokespersons but it is also important for each side to resolve any internal differences before both sides meet, so that each side puts forward a single and agreed view. Producing a single employer or trade union view may require as much discussion and negotiation within each side, as will the achievement of an eventual agreement between the two sides. Frequent adjournments, to enable each side to reconsider their original positions in the light of the points raised during the joint bargaining sessions, are a particular feature of this type of set-piece national negotiation.

The roles of the participants influence their negotiating behaviour. Two types of roles are of particular importance, those of the lay representative and those of the industrial relations professional. Before discussing these, it is worth noting that, except perhaps for the owner-manager of a small business, all the participants act as representatives. They do not negotiate entirely on their own behalf. Managers negotiate as representatives of 'the employer', that is of the corporate body. Trade unionists, whether lay or official, negotiate either on behalf of the union as a collective identity or, more simply, act as representatives of their membership at large. This representative role imparts a degree of detachment or impersonality to the negotiating style. It also acts as a powerful constraint on individual participants' freedom to make claims, offers and concessions. Both parties have to maintain an awareness of the ultimate need for any agreement to achieve the support of the bodies they represent. Middle managers will need to know that top management will accept any compromise they may be minded to agree. Top management want the backing of the Board, and behind the Board stand the shareholders. On the trade union side, a shop steward will need to act in accordance with union policy, or run the risk of losing formal union backing. More broadly, trade union negotiators need to be reasonably confident of being able to secure the acceptance of any proposed agreement by their general membership. Where this is uncertain, they may conclude an agreement on a merely provisional basis, leaving formal acceptance to the votes of the members at large. If the union negotiators consider the agreement a good one, it will be submitted to the membership with a recommendation to accept. In less satisfactory cases, it may be submitted without recommendation, a procedure which leaves less egg on the negotiators' faces if the membership reject the agreement.

As individuals, negotiators on both sides may be either lay or professional. A shop steward is a lay representative; the full-time union organizer or regional or national official is a professional. Industrial relations is his or her full-time occupation. On the management side, the line supervisor or manager acts in a lay capacity. The organization's professional is the personnel or industrial relations manager. The professional's attitude to negotiation is different from the lay person's. To the professional, negotiating is accepted as an integral and important part of the individual's primary occupation. It may well be a favourite and enjoyable part of the job. The lay person, though, may view negotiation as a difficult, stressful and unwelcome addition to an already heavy workload. Of particular interest is the affinity which often develops between the professionals on the two sides. Although, in one sense, the personnel manager and the full-time union official are institutional opponents, they often develop a shared interest – as professional industrial relations practitioners – in ensuring the orderly and effective conduct of negotiations. It is between such professionals that the type of personal working contacts described earlier in this chapter can most readily be established.

References:

[1] THOMASON G. *A textbook of industrial relations management.* London, Institute of Personnel Management. 1984.
[2] KNIVETON B and TOWERS B. *Training for negotiation.* London, Business Books. 1978.
[3] EDWARDES M. *Back from the brink.* London, Collins. 1983.

4 Negotiating strategy

It is unwise to embark on any serious or formal negotiation without considering both the strategy and tactics necessary to secure a satisfactory outcome. Strategy involves the setting of objectives and the planning of the broad approach to be followed. Tactics are the more detailed ploys to be used as negotiation proceeds. This chapter deals with strategy.

Obviously, in any particular negotiation, the strategy has to be specific. In a wage negotiation, for example, it is necessary to consider the top and bottom limits of the company's final position. The assessment of financial objectives is often of critical importance. These specifics are matters for judgement in each individual case, and no detailed guidance can be given in a general text of this kind. What can be suggested, however, are general issues and principles which can be applied to the particular and very different circumstances of almost all negotiations.

These general points can be considered under the following headings:

- Assessing the relative strength of the parties

- Considering whether one's own position can be improved before negotiations begin

- Defining the upper and lower limits of an acceptable outcome

- Considering the probable objectives and approach of the other party

- Deciding what general style and approach to adopt, including timing, the use of pressure or sanctions, the composition of the negotiating team and the roles of its members

- Considering contingency plans should negotiations break down.

Assessing relative strengths

It is common parlance, when discussing a potential negotiation, to speak of each party as being in a strong or weak bargaining position. What is really being discussed is how bargaining power is distributed between the parties – the balance of power.

At its simplest, this is usually based on an assessment of the damage each could do to the other if negotiations failed and there was a resort to coercion. Thus a trade union would be seen as being in a strong position if it seemed that it could effect a strike which would inflict immediate, serious, commercial damage on the employer. Conversely, the employer's position would be described as strong if it seemed probable that the effect of any strike action could be minimized by the existence of large stocks, or by some alternative means of continuing the business. The employer would also be in a strong position if it was judged that circumstances would permit the unilateral imposition of the employer's aims whatever the union's objections might be.

An assessment of the balance of power in these terms is often of critical importance in the planning stage of a negotiation. Is the trade union able to gain ready support from its members for a strike? How damaging would a strike, or some other form of industrial action, be? For how long could such action be experienced before any real financial or commercial crisis arose? How good are the organization's contingency plans for coping with industrial action? Are these plans secure against sympathetic action by employees or trade unions not immediately involved? These are the types of questions to ask.

It must be recognized, though, that the answers will rarely be wholly definitive or objective. As Winkler[1] says: 'The assessment of bargaining power between two parties cannot be measured with tidy calculations. Both parties are dealing with incomplete information about each other. Bargaining is based as much on emotional preferences as on logic.'

Consider, for example, the very common question as to whether or not a workforce would support a strike. It is a matter of judgement. In reaching such a judgement there are, too, several dangers. It is all too easy for hope to triumph over reality, and for a group of managers to talk themselves into believing that the trade union which is threatening strike action is out of touch with its membership. To reach such a conclusion after a couple of chats in the pub with one or two generally compliant employees is the very weak base on which such views are sometimes founded. If such a judgement is then put strongly by a senior manager, it can rapidly become an established view which a better-informed but rather reticent manager may find impossible to challenge.

The opposite danger is too ready an acceptance of strong, repeated and apparently confident, assertions by the trade union officials that: 'The lads are in a very determined mood: if we can't settle soon we won't be able to stop a walk-out.' Of course, this may be true. But it might also be no more than a fairly common bargaining ploy. Knowing which it is, or at least reaching a reasonable assessment of probabilities, may well require extensive sounding out throughout the whole managerial and supervisory group. First-line supervisors, by the very nature of their jobs, are in much closer contact with the workforce at large than are senior managers. Their views are valuable.

Assessments of the balance of power should not be limited to these considerations of the impact of coercive action. There is a need, too, to think about the relative strength of each party within the actual negotiating process. Two particular aspects merit attention – the strength of commitment or determination, and the strength of the actual arguments which will be put forward. One of the reasons why British Leyland continually used to give way to union pressure seems to have been a lack of real determination to establish a managerial bottom line and stick to it. A strike would cause a serious commercial situation, and the management would make a 'final' offer coupled, perhaps, with a threat to close a section or factory if the offer was not accepted. The unions would refuse to accept, and eventually the threat would be set aside and a higher final offer made. In his book on Leyland, Sir Michael Edwardes describes graphically how he set out to change this management attitude, largely by deciding before negotiations started what the outside acceptable limit was and having the determination to stick to it.

So in planning a negotiation, consider how determined the trade union is. Is it an issue on which they would go to the stake? Or are they pressing it mainly because it happens to be national union policy and at local level they need to be seen to have tried something, even if they fail? Consider, too, the management's own position. Is the issue really of critical importance? Or is the trade union's claim being resisted for little better reason than that it has been made? The degree of commitment and determination on each side will be a crucial influence on the conduct and outcome of the negotiation.

Finally, how strong are the actual arguments? Even when the employer is in a strong power position, his negotiating determination will be undermined by a trade union case which is strong in logic or emotion. A classic example of this was in the 1985 negotiations for local government manual workers. This is a very large, low paid group, whose pay position had been slipping for several years as a result of financial constraints on local authority expenditure. Yet few commentators considered that the unions were in a conventionally strong bargaining position. Fear of unemployment or privatization, coupled with the large-scale use of part-time female employment, made it unlikely that the unions could have achieved any rapidly effective industrial action. Despite this, and despite the employers being unable to cope financially with a settlement of much more than three per cent, an actual settlement was concluded after relatively short negotiations of over eight per cent, with more to come from a re-evaluation exercise. How was this achieved? Partly by the unions making a good deal of their plans for disruptive action – the traditional sabre-rattling approach. Partly, too, by their appearing extremely determined to achieve their objective – an impression built up by the whole tenor of their pre-negotiation statements and, later, by their demeanour at the negotiating table. But the real deciding factor was the force of the arguments they put forward which demonstrated the degree to which manual pay had deteriorated relative to other groups, and the extent to which manual employees were having to rely on social security payments to survive on their low take-home pay. As John Edmonds, the unions' principal negotiator described the unions' strategy: 'We set out to establish the case, making the employers feel embarrassed at paying such low rates . . .'[2] What most undermined the employers' original resolve to keep the settlement below five per cent was not the threat of industrial action, it was the persuasive strength of the unions' argument in terms both of logic (the statistics which proved the poor and worsening pay position) and of emotion – the appeal to the employers' sense of fairness.

In planning for a negotiation, this factor needs to be considered. It is difficult psychologically to sustain with enthusiasm and determination a case which is flawed in logic or equity, regardless of the pure power position. It is often easy to identify such flaws in the arguments expected from the other party. It is of equal importance, however, to subject one's own case to critical scrutiny before negotiations commence, rather than have its weaknesses exposed in the course of bargaining.

Strengthening one's own position

After making an initial assessment of the relative strength of the two sides, it is sensible to consider whether one's own position can be improved before negotiations begin. Can the balance of power be altered?

If the main fear is of the effects of possible industrial action it may be feasible to improve matters by such means as:

Letting it be known that a strike at this time would not be wholly unwelcome (provided, of course, that this is the case) as it would enable high product stocks to be cleared; or would achieve savings on wage expenditure at a time when there are outgoing cash flow problems.

Bringing into the open the concern of employees not directly involved that a strike might jeopardize their earnings or jobs, and thus generate pressure on the union in dispute to exercise more caution.

Reminding the trade union of the legal implications of holding a strike without a ballot.

Taking vigorous steps to effect contingency plans designed to ameliorate the impact of a strike, and ensuring that the workforce are aware of this.

Slowing down, or speeding up, the negotiating timetable to ensure that negotiations take place at the most favourable time – for example, after the publication of the latest retail price index if this is expected to show a fall.

Of course, most of these measures could back-fire if used inappropriately. The union will almost certainly understand what is being done, and might treat the employer's action as provocative. It has to be a matter of judgement as to how far this type of pre-negotiation manoeuvring will help or hinder, just as it is in assessing whether union protests about such actions are serious or are merely conventional rhetoric.

In addition to combating possible industrial action, thought should also be given to strengthening one's negotiating case – improving the substance of one's argument. Two particular aspects are worth checking:

Can more information be produced to support the case? This might be statistical (labour turnover, trends in earnings, financial indices) or commercial (sales trends, competitors' plans). It may make use of the power of precedent, referred to in the previous chapter, by the production of evidence of earlier settlements which, it can be claimed, have established agreed principles which should be followed in the current case.

Can useful comparative information be produced about the practice in other plants or organizations? The trade union's case might well be weakened if it can be shown that what it is asking for is well in advance of general standards.

The upper and lower limits

A number of writers on negotiation, particularly when referring to commercial bargaining, suggest that the effective negotiator must have a clear idea about three possible levels of settlement. Kennedy, Benson and Macmillan[3] describe this as the 'L-I-M' approach. L is what the negotiator would like to achieve in ideal circumstances. I is what it is intended to achieve, even if the ideal is unattainable. M is what must be obtained as an absolute minimum. Winkler suggests a similar approach and describes the three levels as the best possible deal, the deal you expect, and the worst (though still just acceptable) deal. All these writers stress the importance of identifying the lowest or bottom line position and sticking to this. Winkler goes a little further and points to the serious commercial risk of being pushed too readily or too often from the middle or target position down to the bottom line.

These commercial concepts are useful in an industrial relations context, subject to one proviso. This is that the commercial and industrial relations parallel breaks down at one point. In almost all commercial transactions, if sticking at the bottom line causes a breakdown in negotiations, the two parties part company. The buyer then looks round for another supplier. The seller similarly goes in search of an alternative customer. That cannot happen in industrial relations. A company and its recognized trade union have a relationship which is more permanent even than marriage. They have to live together and a breakdown in negotiation does not result in the termination of this relationship. In consequence, it is less easy to stick at any pre-determined negotiating point, as the consequences may be worse than one further compromise.

Having said that, it does not follow that the concept of a bottom line should be abandoned. That would be a formula for a steady erosion of the employer's position. What is needed is that in assessing the bottom line a realistic view is taken of the implications of breakdown and a plan, at least in outline, is produced of the consequent action. Whether this involves drastic action such as the closure of a factory, or whether it is related more to the negotiating process such as the use of arbitration or legal action, depends on circumstances. What is important is that if a decision is taken to stick at a particular point – 'not a penny more than six per cent' – thought is also given to what to do next if the union does not agree.

In practice, the most common failure is initially to be too optimistic about the outcome of negotiation and in effect to make the ideal and bottom line objectives coincide. It is far from unknown for a management to go into wage negotiations with one fixed figure in mind, and for this to be based more on hope than realistic judgement. The union rejects this figure out-of-hand in the first ten minutes of negotiation and, because no calculated bottom line exists, the management find themselves pushed into discussing levels of settlement that have not been given adequate prior assessment, and eventually agreeing an outcome which better preparation might have shown was both unacceptable and unnecessary.

The concept of upper and lower limits is not restricted to pay bargaining or to other claims (such as for longer annual leave) which are quantified. Consider, for example, a dispute over the dismissal of a shop steward for continued disruptive action in breach of procedure agreements. The ideal outcome from the management's point of view will be that the steward stays sacked with no concessions of any kind having been made. But if it is seen that the steward has significant employee support, and that the union considers that certain wider principles are at stake, some concessions might be worth considering. The bottom line might be that the steward is not sacked, but is barred from holding a shop steward appointment. Or perhaps that he or she stays sacked, but that a new procedure is introduced in which the full-time union officials are given a greater involvement in the disciplining of shop stewards.

The general point to bear in mind is that unless there is a very good chance of the single, ideal outcome being achieved, then fall-back positions need to be identified if negotiations are not either to founder, or to be conducted in a dangerously unplanned manner.

The success of a negotiation in the sense of achieving a desirable or at least satisfactory outcome, is dependent on making a correct analysis of what such a level of settlement would be. Setting such objectives may require considerable research into the benefits and disbenefits of alternative negotiating strategies. In a commercial situation, statistical analyses of the effects of different possible settlements on unit costs, pricing and profitability are essential.

Assessing the other party's case

There is more to the preparation for negotiation than assessing, and perhaps altering, the balance of power. It is also of critical importance to consider what the other party's real objectives are and how, in the course of bargaining and argument, it is likely to try to achieve them.

It may be thought that its objectives are obvious: quite simply, just what it is asking for. But, in reality, things may not be so straightforward. Suppose, for example, that the trade union is claiming an increase in basic wage rates. That may appear to be the union's obvious and only objective. It is worth considering, however, whether the real issue is the level of take-home earnings. If so, then the door might be open to some progress by way of enhanced productivity payments or higher overtime premia – alternatives which in some circumstances might be more acceptable from a management viewpoint.

Take another example. The union is demanding the dismissal of a

39

supervisor who has allegedly been using racial abuse in dealings with employees from an ethnic minority. Management may be very reluctant to take such severe action against a long-service foreman, particularly as this might result in a counter dispute with the supervisors as a group. Is dismissal really the union's primary objective? Perhaps their real concern is that the company has never made it clear to the supervisors that racist behaviour is unacceptable and is a potential disciplinary matter. Perhaps an acceptable solution would be the introduction of general instructions and guidelines for all managerial and supervisory staff, coupled with a warning to the offending individual.

It is always worth while to look behind the overt objective of the other party to see if there is not some hidden agenda, some wider point or principle which the negotiation should more constructively address. Occasionally, too, the reverse situation may arise. A trade union may, for example, say that it wants to raise the whole general procedure for allocating overtime. Before plunging into what might be an expensive negotiation on a matter affecting all employees, it is wise to check that there has not been one particular incident which might be susceptible to individual attention at far less potential cost. Personnel managers are often asked by other managers: 'What is the company policy about x, y or z?' The experienced personnel manager's reply is: 'Tell me about your problem.' It often transpires that the real issue is an individual case which may or may not be assisted by an explanation of the apparently relevant general policy. Checking on what has triggered a general claim or complaint by a trade union often reveals a similarly individual issue. Of course, the trade union may be using this as an opportunity to exploit the broader point, but if management shows that it has identified the individual trigger, and is prepared to do something about it, this may well reduce the effectiveness of the union's general claim.

It is also helpful, if at all possible, to obtain information in advance of a negotiating meeting, of the actual case or arguments which the trade union will be putting forward. In very formal negotiations, such as set-piece national pay bargaining, the submission of a written case obviously facilitates such pre-negotiation assessment. Such written statements often make much use of statistical data, and all such figures need to be checked as to the validity of their sources, and to spot if any statistical tricks have been used. A trade union claiming a massive pay increase for one particular skilled occupation made much play in its case statement of annual labour turnover running at 100 per cent in one plant. A quick check showed that only two such employees worked at that plant and, by a coincidence, both had left in the previous 12 months, one on retirement, the other on medical grounds.

Where written case statements are not part of the normal procedure, it may still be possible to obtain a good deal of prior information about the trade union's case. One means of doing so is wholly informal. If the personnel manager has established a good working relationship with the relevant trade union official, it may be possible to conduct some off-the-record soundings on a person to person basis. Slightly more formally, consider the example of the full-time union official who writes to the chief executive requesting an early meeting to discuss 'the very unsatisfactory situation regarding the use of sub-contractors in your head office rebuilding project'. This merits a letter from the personnel manager along these lines:

> Thank you for your recent letter to the chief executive, asking for a meeting to discuss the use of sub-contractors. He has asked me to explain that his diary is very heavily booked for the next couple of weeks and it would be difficult to find a date for a meeting until early next month. To avoid any undue delay, and to ensure that when the meeting does take place it will be possible to come to an immediate conclusion about any points you raise, it would be very helpful if you could let me have a note, setting out the issues you wish to discuss, together with any facts or proposals which you would like us to consider. Alternatively, you may prefer to have an informal preliminary meeting with me at which we can go over the issues which you would like to raise with the chief executive. Perhaps you could telephone my office to let me know which of these courses of action you would prefer.

Whichever option the trade union official chooses will enable the management to learn more about the case before any formal negotiation takes place. If the union official sends in a more detailed letter, that will provide time for some research or discussion on the management side. If, more probably, the suggestion of an informal meeting is chosen, this will give the personnel manager an opportunity not just to find the substance of the trade union's case, but also to settle the matter if it transpires that the issues lie within the authority of the personnel manager to decide.

Deciding the style and approach

Having made a thorough assessment of the other side's position, it is time to plan how, if possible, the negotiation should proceed. Clearly this is not wholly open to one side's decisions. A plan to spin out the negotiations over the longest possible time period may, in the event, be frustrated by the strategies adopted by the other party. But to go into negotiations with no thought at all having been given to their preferred timing, style and format is a recipe for failure.

Timing, or the pace of negotiation, is often of major importance. If a dispute has blown up very quickly on a highly emotional issue – perhaps, a fatal accident at work or a dismissal – it may well be of advantage to slow the pace of discussion in order to allow time for the initially highly charged atmosphere to subside. Effective negotiations are rarely possible when emotion and sentiment are running high. Achieving some delay in such circumstances needs very careful handling. It is all too easy to make the situation worse by acting in a way which gives the impression of callousness or irresponsibility. One wholly justified and often very desirable method is to persuade the trade union of the necessity of a fact-finding enquiry before any constructive discussion is possible.

In other circumstances, delay may increase the cost of the eventual settlement. This sometimes occurs in wage bargaining. The union claims eight per cent; the employer does not wish to agree more than four per cent, though the union is in a position to inflict considerable financial damage if the negotiations become deadlocked. In such circumstances it is probably unwise to spin out the process of bargaining by first offering four and a half per cent and then going through a long process of offers being turned down, marginally improved offers being made (five, six, six and a half per cent etc), followed by counter claims. The union's resolve may well be strengthened by what they perceive as delaying tactics, and the final position may well be a choice of paying seven per cent or of a breakdown leading to a damaging strike. A quick offer of, say, five and a half per cent, supported by the provision of full financial information to show how difficult any higher figure would be, might well be a better strategy. It will result in a better deal for management, while the trade union also may well see a benefit for its members in a quickly concluded settlement which avoids the possibility of the hardship caused by strike action. Trade unions have as good reasons for the prevention of strikes as employers.

The use of pressure or sanctions as a means of changing the balance of power, or as measures to consider if negotiations fail, has been discussed earlier in this and the preceding chapter. The relevance of the topic here is to the style of negotiation which is appropriate to the circumstances of each case.

At the two extremes, should the style be relaxed, friendly and open; or assertive and confrontational? The answer is rarely clear-cut and, in negotiations of any complexity, elements of both these extremes may be appropriate at different stages. Nevertheless, it is still important to consider the overall characteristic, even if within this general style, bargaining episodes will occur in which a contrasting approach may be needed.

The two extremes just mentioned should not be confused with weakness or strength. Given a strong bargaining position, it is not necessarily desirable to adopt an abrupt, confrontational stance. Indeed, if it is expected that the trade union will eventually have to swallow the bitter pill of a settlement far below its original claim, there may be a strong case for leading them into this position by a process of gentle explanation and persuasion, rather than by rubbing their noses in their obvious defeat. Relationships have to be maintained into the future, and the avoidance of deep-seated resentment might well be one of the management's objectives in these circumstances.

Conversely, negotiators sometimes feel that a weak case can be strengthened by adopting an assertive stance, though the danger of having one's bluff called must be given serious thought. Slightly more subtle is the point that it is sometimes worth letting the other side gain the impression that they have had to work hard for whatever outcome they achieve.

The style to adopt needs to reflect the characteristics and experience of the other side's negotiators. Generalizing, the more experienced the negotiators, the less they will be thrown off balance by a confrontational stance. As an example, consider a management's response to a claim for a 32 hour week, submitted in the context of a package of claims, in one instance by a newly elected and very inexperienced committee of office staff representatives, and in another instance by a highly experienced full-time trade union officer.

The management's response to the office committee might be along these lines, taking a firm, no-nonsense stand:

> Before we talk about the important parts of your claim, we'll have to dispose of this very odd suggestion for a 32 hour week. It is wholly out of line with general practice in the industry, would be wildly expensive and could jeopardize the whole business and all your jobs. There is absolutely no possibility of making any concessions on working hours, and unless we can forget this particular point we might as well close the meeting now!

This very firm, dismissive approach might well panic the inexperienced office representatives into hastily agreeing that they would not wish this item to prejudice discussion on the rest of their case.

It is highly improbable that this abrupt approach would work with the experienced, professional trade union negotiator. Starting negotiations with an attempt to knock the other party off balance is something of a negotiating cliché so far as professionals are concerned. A more effective style here would be to open the discussion far more cautiously, leaving considerable room for manoeuvre. The management's response might be:

> Before we get onto other parts of the claim, it might be helpful if you could say a bit more about the 32 hour week. Frankly, we find this a bit puzzling. We checked around the industry last week and as we are sure you know, it would be way out of line with current practice. You've obviously thought, too, about the financial implications which would make it difficult for us to be very constructive about other parts of your claim. So perhaps you could help us by explaining more clearly why you think we should go this far, and how this item ranks in your members' priorities.

This less direct or forceful approach gets a similar message across, but without provocation. It also places the ball back in the other side's court, though this is a matter more of tactics (dealt with in the next chapter) than of strategy.

Planning for negotiation should also include decisions about the composition of the management's negotiating team and the roles of its members. The more detailed aspects of this are referred to in the next chapter, but on a strategic basis there are two main issues to consider – the size of the team, and whether it should have one or more tiers.

Trade unions tend towards fairly large negotiating teams in other than informal shop steward to supervisor situations. This is not because large teams are more effective. It usually stems either from more than one union being involved or from the constitutional need for a number of union representatives to be seen to be involved or simply from a feeling of strength in numbers. The greater the emphasis the union places on the concept of its officials acting only on the authority and decisions of the membership, the more likely it is that they will have to field a large negotiating team, usually a mix of full-time officers and lay elected representatives.

There is no need for managements to think that they should match the union team for size, nor to consider that to field a much smaller team will place the management in a weak position. Indeed, the reverse may be true. The larger the team, the greater the likelihood of individual members forming differing views in the course of discussion, and the greater the difficulty in keeping to a consistent and coherent line of argument.

This is not to say, however, that the ideal number is one. Negotiation demands a high level of concentration and quick thinking, and it is very difficult for one person to maintain 100 per cent attention to everything that is said, and to detect every nuance in complex discussions. It would be wrong to claim that any one size of team was in all circumstances ideal. Nevertheless, writers on the subject and many experienced negotiators indicate a preference for between three and five. A smaller number may make the pressure on individuals too great; a larger number and there are risks that the other side may be able to open up and exploit differences of view.

Negotiations may be handled at more than one tier or level. In many cases, a disputes or collective bargaining agreement may specify such levels and thus prevent any choice. The agreement may, for example, set out a three tier system in which unresolved issues move up from the shop floor, where line managers are involved, to the personnel manager, to the chief executive. Where such levels are not specified it

45

is always worth considering whether or not to handle a negotiation on a phased and 'tiered' basis.

An example was given earlier in this chapter of a union seeking a meeting with the chief executive, but the matter being dealt with in the first instance by the personnel manager. The main reason for that approach in that example was to obtain prior information about the union's case. Another reason would be to prolong the negotiations. There is also another reason – the possible value of avoiding what might be an early breakdown by keeping another level of negotiation in reserve. If it looks as though the negotiation could be difficult, and if the avoidance of confrontation is an objective, it may be a sensible strategy to divide the negotiating team into two (exceptionally more) tiers. The first round of bargaining might then be handled by the personnnel manager, one of his or her senior staff and a relevant line manager. If they fail to achieve a settlement, the negotiations could then be moved up to a team consisting of the chief executive, a senior line manager and the personnel manager. Psychologically, as well as strategically, a change of level of this kind facilitates changes of approach, or agreement to compromises, which if occurring within a single team would be perceived as involving defeat or a loss of face.

There are also advantages in allocating different roles to different team members. In a team of three, for example, one will act as the negotiating leader and probably act in a primarily constructive, reasonable and at times conciliatory manner. Another member will take the hard-line role. He or she will challenge the union's assertions and emphasize the difficulty of going anywhere near meeting the union's claims. The third member can act as 'sweeper', observing the reactions of all the members of the union's team and picking up any signs of differences of view. He or she may also keep a check on the points being made by the other two members of the management team, and bring in anything the other two may have omitted. Again, how this is done is more a matter of tactics than strategy. At the strategic planning level what is important is to sort out the general nature and allocation of these roles before negotiations commence.

Contingency planning

Reference has been made earlier to planning to ameliorate the effects of industrial action in the event of a breakdown in negotiations. But strike action is not the inevitable outcome of a negotiating deadlock and there are other aspects of contingency planning which need to be considered.

The most important of these is the possible use of third party assistance through conciliation or arbitration using either the Advisory Conciliation and Arbitration Service (ACAS) or some other external organization or person. This is the subject of Chapter 9 and is therefore not discussed in detail here. The general point which needs to be thought about in the planning phase is just what line should be followed if the negotiations become deadlocked. Of course, if there is a dispute agreement which already lays down that conciliation or arbitration shall be used, then that is that and no decision has to be made. But in the absence of such a procedure agreement it is as well to give the matter serious thought.

Given deadlock, will the strategy be to dig in and fight the matter out, or to seek outside aid, and if so what type of aid? The answer to this may well influence the actual bargaining strategy. If the dispute may have to end in a battle, then bargaining compromises can be taken right down to the employer's absolute bottom line. But if it is thought advisable to seek conciliation or arbitration, then it needs to be recognized that these processes normally involve some further movement from the position reached at deadlock. That may indicate the need for caution in negotiation in order to leave some room for other than catastrophic further movement after negotiations have failed.

References

[1] WINKLER J. *Bargaining for results*. London, Heinemann. 1981.
[2] 'Man of the Moment'. *Personnel Management*, January 1986. pp 18–19.

5 Negotiating tactics: I

The tactics of negotiation are the various gambits, ploys, methods and modes of behaviour which, if adopted with care and skill, help to bring a negotiation to an effective conclusion. They are therefore concerned with movement from a position in which the two parties hold different or opposing views, to one in which agreement is reached. From either party's viewpoint, the most satisfactory agreement is one which is as close as possible to their opening position. Tactics are therefore concerned with trying to gain maximum movement from the other party, while conceding as little as possible oneself. In an industrial relations context this may seem an unacceptably manipulative or commercial approach. Good industrial relations involve far more than being smarter than the trade unions in collective bargaining. If this chapter appears to ignore these wider issues it is because managerial weakness in negotiating does not aid the formation of sound industrial relations, and because the long-term effects of any negotiation should be considered before bargaining starts and within the strategic planning phase dealt with in the last chapter; with tactics being modified accordingly. One warning note can be sounded here. It is that to be seen to be too devious, too clever, in handling negotiations, will make it difficult to establish the constructive type of working relationship with trade union representatives which this book considers a pre-condition both of effective negotiation and of good industrial relations. Negotiation can also be considered very broadly as falling into two phases. In the first, on which this chapter concentrates, the two parties set out to try to defend or strengthen their different positions. In the second, the phase covered in the next chapter, a more collaborative process occurs as the two parties seek to find common ground and so reach agreement.

The literature on negotiation provides a multiplicity of advice, hints and tips about tactics. They can be grouped as follows:

48

The physical arrangements: numbers of participants, location, seating, refreshments, documentation

Defining the issues: setting the scene, clarifying the two positions

Probing the other party's case: exposing flaws, undermining the leader's credibility

Strengthening one's own case: hard and soft line tactics, introducing or excluding other issues, attaching conditions to concessions, the use and misuse of emotion

Timing: the use of adjournments, bargaining to exhaustion

Searching for common ground: looking for links between the two cases, reading between the lines, talking and listening

Working towards agreement: helping the other party move, the use of humour, avoiding loss of face, periodic summaries, hypothetical suggestions, constructive compromise

Defining and clinching the agreement: the use and misuse of 'fudge', closing the agreement, ensuring full understanding, ending on a high note, producing immediate written confirmation.

Each of the detailed points within these eight stages is now examined more fully.

Numbers of participants

Deciding on the size and composition of the management team is an important point of strategy, as discussed in the last chapter. Tactically, thought should also be given to the size of the trade union team. If the objective, in terms of style, is to have an informal, exploratory discussion rather than a formal bargaining session, but the trade union says it wishes to field a full-time official plus the 10-person shop stewards' committee, then something needs to be changed. Either a formal session will have to be accepted, or the leader of the trade union side persuaded that there might be an advantage in changing the format of the meeting, perhaps to a one-to-one discussion with the personnel manager. In the formal setting, the trade union should not necessarily be discouraged from fielding a large team. As suggested in the last chapter, this may weaken their negotiating position by opening up the possibility of differences of view occurring which the management side will be able to exploit.

Location

There may be a choice of location for the negotiating meeting – perhaps between a manager's office and some more neutral ground such as a conference room within the organization or, even more neutral, a room in a hotel. Numbers, of course, may determine this, as may custom and practice. It is very common for national negotiations to be based in a hotel or other commercial conference suite. When a choice does exist, there is sometimes an advantage in choosing managerial home ground, such as the chief executive's office. With fully experienced negotiators on both sides the location should make little difference. But inexperienced managers may feel more confident in their own office environment, while inexperienced lay union representatives may be somewhat overawed by the, to them, rarified aura of the chief executive's suite or the boardroom. Against this, if the management wishes to demonstrate its open and even-handed approach, a suggestion to the trade union that the meeting might best be held off the home territory can be a useful ploy. It often results in the union saying they are happy to meet in a management office!

Seating arrangements

How the participants are seated can have a significant effect on the quality of discussion. There is a good deal of anecdotal and research evidence to show that collaborative discussion is enhanced by people sitting next to each other, while if they sit facing each other across the table then the discussion tends to be more competitive or confrontational. The conventional layout for a negotiating meeting is the latter. The management team sits on one side of the table with their leading spokesperson in the middle: they are faced across the table by the trade union side whose leader will likewise sit at the centre and opposite the management leader. A common alternative, particularly when the management team is smaller than the trade union's, is for the senior manager to sit at the head of the table flanked by his supporting colleagues, and for the union representatives to sit around the other three sides of the table. In such a layout it is interesting to note that the trade union leader will normally choose to sit in the centre of the other short side of the table, opposite the management spokesperson.

Either of these layouts is wholly appropriate to a conventional, hard-bargaining session. Seating the leaders of the two sides opposite one another is particularly helpful in this type of situation because it aids the direct, eye to eye contact which is essential to effective interpersonal discussion. There may be cases, however, when it would be worth while thinking of breaking away from this standard, somewhat confrontational, format. It is certainly not appropriate, for example, to any form of joint management/union working party. But even in the negotiating mode, a different pattern of seating may be helpful. Suppose, for instance, that it seems likely that the full-time union official will adopt a fairly aggressive stance, while the senior steward or lay representative is known to have more conciliatory leanings. It might then be worth engineering an unorthodox seating plan. The management spokesman might sit at one corner of the table, with one of his or her colleagues opposite, blocking off the confrontational position. The other management representative(s) can also leave a seating gap from these two. They would all take up these positions before the union side enter the room. As the union representatives enter, the management leader waves to the senior steward to come and sit in the neighbouring corner chair, while another manager – perhaps the personnel manager – beckons the full-time official to sit alongside and out of the line of sight of the management spokesperson. The stage is then set for a discussion in which the full-time official will have great difficulty in acting as an effective leader, while the management leader is able to talk directly to the senior steward.

Anyone who doubts the impact of seating plans should try an unconventional arrangement of this kind and then observe the consternation on the faces of the trade union or the management representatives when they are invited to sit other than in a solid and opposing phalanx.

Refreshments

Providing coffee or tea, or in longer sessions beer and sandwiches, has become part of the ritual of negotiations. It is expected of the management side and to omit to do so will be taken as a far greater indication of meanness than the inexperienced manager may realize. 'The bastards rejected our claim without even giving us a cup of tea!'

The refreshment break can, however, be used for other purposes than complying with ritual or just being normally courteous. It is as well to keep control of its timing. It is very unhelpful for someone to arrive with the tea just as a delicate possibility of a compromise is being explored. So the management leader should pick the right time by using a buzzer to the outside office, or by signalling to one of his colleagues to go and summon refreshments. The break can be used to lower the temperature if the argument is getting overheated. It creates an impersonal reason for a pause, during which tempers can abate and individual conversations take place which may help to clear the air. More deviously, and only if the refreshments can be called for unobtrusively, their arrival might just happen to occur as the trade union leader is in mid argument and leading up to a powerful peroration.

Delaying their arrival may also sometimes be effective in encouraging the meeting to make progress, the management leader might say: 'We've laid on beer and sandwiches for lunch, but I think we ought to deal with x or y before we break, otherwise we may well lose the thread of our arguments.' x and y, of course, are sticky points on which the management want to keep up the pressure for a quick and favourable settlement. If the management side have prepared this ploy (including having had a sandwich just before the meeting began at 10 30) the trade union side will be getting very restless by 14 15 if the discussion on x or y has still not been concluded.

Documentation

This is primarily a question of minutes – are they to be kept, if so by whom and in what form? As noted earlier, this is sometimes laid down within formal procedure agreements. For example, in the Burnham Committee (the forum for teachers' national negotiations) it was deemed necessary some years ago to keep a verbatim record and shorthand writers have consequently been producing voluminous records of every word spoken, however irrelevant or incoherent some of the contributions to the debates have been. The reason was the difficulty which was experienced in getting the two somewhat distrustful parties to agree any more normal form of summarized minutes, compounded by bad relationships within the multi-union side with consequent disputes about who had said what.

In more normal circumstances, verbatim records cannot be recommended. The important thing about any effective negotiation is its product – the agreement that is produced – not the process of negotiation itself. There is consequently a good deal to be said for a minute which does little more than record who was present, a brief summary of the opening positions, and what was eventually agreed.

This type of minute does not require a formal note-taker. Provided the management team sort this out before the negotiation begins, one of their team can be deputed to produce a note of the meeting and, if requested or otherwise considered desirable, clear this in draft with his or her opposite number before it goes onto the official record.

It may be helpful for the management to keep a fuller private record. This again would have to be the task of one of the management representatives, normally the personnel manager. It would record, in a complex negotiation, the possibly differing views or emphases of different members of the trade union side, together with a note of those ideas or proposals which emerged in discussion but did not eventually figure in the final agreement. If a private note of this kind is kept, it should never be used openly in a later negotiation. It should be no more than an aid to managerial memory, not a secret weapon to be used to throw the other side into confusion in the course of a subsequent dispute.

If both sides agree that a fuller minute is needed it may be necessary to arrange for the attendance of a skilled note-taker – not an easy task if many hours of convoluted argument have to be summarized in a way which does justice to every participant. This is certainly not a task which should be saddled on any of the management team. It is not possible to play an effective bargaining role while attempting to make detailed notes. An alternative might be to tape-record the proceedings, though this cannot be recommended with any enthusiasm. Unless the room is equipped for this purpose the quality of the recording will probably be appalling. Some unfortunate note-taker will also have to sit through hours of playback, with the added difficulty of trying to identify the various speakers, and without all the visual cues of gesture and facial expression to distinguish the flippant from the serious.

Setting the scene

The first main speaker in a negotiation has a considerable influence on the substance and character of the subsequent discussion. He or she will state what the main issues are, while the speaker's style – friendly or aggressive – will probably be echoed by subsequent speakers on both sides. The trade union will often have the advantage here. In many cases the negotiation will be taking place to consider a trade union claim or complaint. The proportion of meetings initiated by management will probably be smaller. If, as is customary, the party whose case triggered the meeting is given the first word, this means that the trade union will in the majority of instances have the advantage of this scene-setting role.

There is a way of avoiding this without openly breaking the normal convention. Assume, for example, that the union has submitted a claim for higher car allowances while the management would like to avoid any immediate increase in such costs. Conventionally, management would open the meeting by turning to the spokesperson for the union team and saying: 'We are meeting to consider your claim, so perhaps you would like to start.' Whereupon the union speaker can launch into a well prepared argument, adopting whatever tone is considered best.

The alternative, which in effect gives management the first word and the opportunity to influence the tone of the meeting, is for the management leader to start along these lines: 'We are meeting to consider your claim, so I am sure you would like to bat first. But before we start, I would find it helpful just to run over the background to this subject so that we are all in the same picture.' Note the phrase 'before we start'. This should prevent an immediate objection about the management getting in first. Note, too, that in this example it is the management's intention to create a helpful, informal atmosphere. The way is now open for the manager to run over the history of the current car allowance arrangements and perhaps to drop a hint that the management, too, are not very happy with them, and that a joint study of alternative ways of providing business transport might be worth considering, particularly if this could identify a more cost-effective system.

Provided the management leader keeps this allegedly pre-meeting introduction fairly short, the trade union side will probably not have time to react and object; although the union's planned approach may well have been thrown completely off course.

Clarifying the two positions

Before effective bargaining can begin, and after any preliminary skirmishing of the kind just discussed, it is important that each side develops a clear view of the other's position. This is often an important factor when the meeting is called, not to deal with a clearly specified trade union claim, but rather with a union complaint about some alleged managerial malpractice, or about poor working conditions. The union will demand a meeting to discuss, say, the high frequency of headaches and other symptoms of tension among computer room staff. There is likely to come a point in this discussion when the management need to say: 'We now have a clear idea about what is troubling your members in the computer room: but what are you asking us actually to do about it?'

It is also important that the trade union side clearly understands the management's position. It is all too easy for a barren argument to develop, simply because of misunderstanding or confusion resulting from a poorly explained management case. The same advice can apply here as is often given to public speakers: 'Tell them what you are going to say; say it; then tell them what you have said.' In the course of discussion, too, if the other side appears to be missing the point, stop arguing and say: 'There may be some confusion here. Are you clear that the key point we are making is x?' Similarly, if there is some doubt about the union's case, ask: 'Are we right in thinking that the point you want us to consider is y?' Asking questions often leads to better progress than making statements.

Exposing flaws

It is a normal phenomenon for each side to be convinced by the force of its own argument. It is therefore necessary to attempt to sap this confidence by exposing any flaws in the other party's case. These may be errors of fact, or the misuse of statistics, or errors of logic, particularly the drawing of conclusions from an unsound base. This is best achieved by asking questions; questions are less provocative than assertions and tend to put the other party on the defensive. Assume the common practice of quoting an 'average' figure for a fairly small number of cases without explaining whether this is the arithmetic mean, the median, or less probably the mode. The management side may know that the arithmetic mean has been used in some earnings statistics being used by the trade union, and that this is wildly misleading because of one or two cases which are way out of line with the general trend. It is tempting to sail straight in with a scornful comment that: 'Your so-called average is really meaningless', and then going on to rebut it with the use of the more realistic median.

It is more effective to draw out from the other side how their average was calculated and to get them to produce the alternative and better figure. So the approach might be: 'We're interested in your figure for average earnings. Could we look at the list of actual earnings on which it is based? How many cases are there in this list? Do you see that two of the 15 are very much higher than all the others? What's the figure at the mid-point of the list?'

The more one can persuade the other party to talk, the more likelihood there is of spotting flaws. The initial statements of the principal speakers will probably have been carefully prepared, with any cracks in fact or logic skilfully papered over. If the supporting members of the other side's team can be drawn into the discussion, and their leader asked to explain their case in a different sequence to the opening presentation, it is probable that sooner or later weaknesses will be found in what initially seemed to be a well-structured argument.

Undermining credibility

It would be wrong to suggest that in all negotiations an attempt should

56

be made to undermine the credibility of the other side's leader. If his or her standing in the eyes of the whole trade union side is justifiably high, any attempt at belittlement could be wholly counterproductive.

But it is not unknown for the leader to be in that position, not so much on intellect, integrity and ability, as on a facility for speaking in a forceful manner on a public platform, or on the outcome of a personal or political power struggle. In these circumstances, particularly if it is thought that the other members of the union team have some doubts about the strength of their case, it is worth an attempt to pin any flaws in that case on their leader personally, and so sap their• side's confidence in the person they have been following.

The leader may be a full-time official, the rest of the team being lay representatives. They will obviously look to this official as an expert on, say the legal aspects of their case. In arguing the case, the official might quote an Employment Appeal Tribunal decision. The personnel manager spots that this decision has just been overturned by the House of Lords and can then say: 'You would be right, George, except that you're out of date in your case law. Didn't you know that the House of Lords overturned that EAT ruling last week? If you like, I'll show you *The Times* law report.' An incident of this kind will begin to sow doubt in the minds of the lay representatives as to whether their leader is as competent and well-informed as they may have thought.

Hard and soft line tactics

Whether the overall tenor of one's case should be hard or soft has already been discussed as a strategic issue. Choosing when to use these different styles within that overall approach is a matter of tactics. Experience indicates that the occasional use of a contrasting style in either direction can be a most effective way of concluding one stage in negotiation and starting another. It is rather like a psychological gear-change. Say the general tenor has been friendly, relaxed, exploratory and discursive. Discussion is just about to move onto a new point. The management leader says: 'On this issue the position is very different. We find your claim to be wholly unrealistic, completely unreasonable and very obviously totally unacceptable. We are sorry that you have spoilt an otherwise responsible claim with so peculiar a proposal and I hope we can now move onto your next point on which I am sure we will be able to have a constructive discussion.' There is obviously a risk here of very adverse reaction, but also a good chance – if the management have judged things shrewdly – of the cold shock of a sudden change of style making the union side realize that on this issue the management are 100 per cent determined not to budge.

A similar sudden change, this time from a generally hard to a soft line, would be appropriate as a signal that there is a deal to be done at that particular stage.

Introducing or excluding new issues

Situations will arise within a negotiation when one or other party raises an issue which has not figured in the formal case statements or was not expected when the meeting was arranged. A rule of thumb on this practice is: if the new issue will help to achieve a settlement, bring it in or accept it – if not, don't raise it or if the other party does, try to exclude it.

For example, take the union's claim for higher car allowances referred to earlier. From a management viewpoint, there may be an advantage in bringing in several other issues – perhaps car leasing, the use of public transport and even subsistence allowances. The trade union will want the negotiation limited to their one topic. It will be a matter of negotiating skill as to whether the management will succeed in diluting this claim by introducing the other issues. In this example, these other points are all of some relevance to the basic subject. They may enable an agreement to be reached on a package of issues instead of on a single topic, and the packaging of issues provides much more scope for compromise and trade-offs between different elements than the more intense bargaining which tends to develop on a single issue.

There is another use of additional issues, of items which are peripheral or even irrelevant to the original point. This is a defensive ploy, used to create a diversion or breathing space when the going gets uncomfortably rough. The bargaining may be about an increase in annual leave, and the union may have the management side on the run by showing how far behind the industry's norm are the company's current provisions. The management leader then says: 'Before we go any further I have to say that this opens up the whole question of our worsening quality standards.' (This is not the key issue, but measures are called for to stop the management position sliding.) 'We really can't go on talking about more leisure time, how we might all take life easier, when what this company dearly needs is much more commitment to high standards while we are at work!' No union negotiator of any experience would swallow this, but one or two members of the union team may not be able to resist the temptation to follow the subsidiary issues and so interrupt the flow of negotiation, just at a point when this was working against the management.

The converse position applies when the other side attempts the same tactics. One quite common ploy used by trade union officials is to introduce a personal comment or attack instead of answering an awkward management point. So the union official's response to the personnel manager who has just pointed out a flaw in the union's interpretation of the law might be: 'That's just the sort of clever point we've come to expect from this management. As soon as we suggest something which would help our members to have slightly better conditions – and God knows, they need improvement – up pops Mr Smith with some cold legal jargon which he says prevents you doing anything. Why don't you say what you really think, Mr Smith, which is that you think we're a crowd of ignorant peasants who don't deserve anything better!' It may take much self control not to react in kind – but if the negotiating point is not to be lost, this type of intervention must not be allowed to divert attention from the real issues.

Attaching conditions to concessions

This is one of the most important principles of negotiation. In commercial negotiations it may almost be taken as a universal rule that there should be no concessions without conditions. Get something back for anything which you have to concede even if, because of an unequal power position, the condition may not have the same value as the concession.

In industrial relations it is not possible to go quite this far. In a simple wage negotiation, for example, a move from six per cent to six and a half per cent may be necessary to get a settlement and it may not be possible to tie any conditions to this move, or to find any sort of trade-off.

Such conditions or trade-offs should, however, always be sought, and the principle should be abandoned only when it is very evident that nothing more can be achieved. How can conditions best be introduced? Two things are important. Mention the condition first and the concession next. Do not give details of the concession until there is an indication that the condition is at least negotiable. Take a negotiation about a package of claims by a trade union which includes a shorter working week and longer annual leave. Assuming the management is willing to consider some movement on total working time, this part of the negotiation might start with the management leader saying: 'If you are prepared to set aside a change in the working week, we might feel able to talk about annual leave.' The condition, abandoning the claim for a shorter working week, is put first, so the concession is clearly conditional. The size of the possible concession has not been detailed, partly to avoid creating too early a benchmark, partly to see whether there is any likelihood of the condition being accepted before any commitments can be claimed to have been made.

This principle may be used to justify the introduction of completely new issues, as discussed a little earlier. So in the apparently simple, single issue wage negotiation, the possibility of a move from six per cent to six and a half per cent might be introduced by the management saying: 'If we were to consider going any further than the six per cent which you have just rejected, we would have to bring forward a proposal which we had not intended raising until much later this year – the need to start up a Saturday shift worked by part-timers instead of paying weekend overtime.' This might not work – but it is always worth thinking of possible trade-offs for any negotiating concessions or compromise.

The use and misuse of emotion

The general rule of negotiating is that it is best to avoid becoming emotionally committed. It is difficult to be imaginative and flexible in considering alternative options if one has a deep, personalized commitment to a single position. It is also dangerous to rise to the bait of a personal attack, however natural such an emotional response might be. Generally speaking, effective negotiating calls for a cool head and an absence of personalized comment or argument. It is the issues which should be concentrated on, not personal dignity or the sheer enjoyment of scoring debating points.

Having said that, for some people in some circumstances a display of emotion, provided it is wholly sincere and not out of proportion to the scale of the issue under discussion, may be beneficial to both the tenor and content of the negotiation. Suppose, for example, that the whole quality of discussion has degenerated to bad-tempered exchanges on points of minor detail. The position might well be rescued by a respected member of either side making a very personal and deeply felt appeal for a cessation of such squabbling and a reversion to a responsible discussion of ways forward.

Similarly, if a trade union speaker makes a serious but unfounded attack on the integrity of the management side or one of its members, it may be appropriate to respond with a passionate rebuttal, linked with a strongly worded reminder that no real progress is likely unless each side respects the other's sincerity. This should not be the response to a mere diversionary attack which would be better ignored, but is justified if the trade union speaker's allegations are meant seriously and seem to be adversely influencing the whole interactive process of constructive discussion between the two sides.

Adjournments

Adjournments to enable one or both sides to reconsider their positions in private are very much a normal part of the ritual of large-scale national negotiations. The trade union makes its opening statement and claim. The employers, who have already seen this case set out in the union's written submission, make their prepared response, the trade union gives its first reply to the employers' opening statement, the employers respond with their first very tentative indication of areas for possible movement. There is then an adjournment during which each side reviews the position and prepares the next couple of moves.

Adjournments are just as useful in smaller scale and less formal negotiations. They can serve at least three purposes:

1   To give the parties an opportunity to reconsider the progress and objectives of the negotiation.

2   To provide a break if the negotiations have reached an impasse or

have become bogged down in trivia or in personal argument. It is surprising how much the atmosphere can change for the better after a 20 minute break.

3 To provide an opportunity for one or two members of each side to talk with each other away from the bargaining table and explore possible ways forward in a very informal manner which would not be possible in the formal bargaining arena.

These 'corridor talks' during adjournments, often between the personnel manager and the union's principal negotiator, may well be the most productive way of achieving progress where there are two large bargaining teams. These two participants share an interest as professionals in making progress and avoiding breakdown. In the privacy of the corridor (actual or metaphoric) they can take soundings on a confidential and no-commitment basis which is quite impossible in the context of formal discussions between two large teams. They need the convention of an adjournment to rationalize the process. They also need to respect each other's integrity and confidence.

Bargaining to exhaustion

It is something of a media myth that tough employers win negotiating battles with trade unions by keeping the bargaining going into the small hours of the morning, and so wearing down the union negotiators' resolve by sheer exhaustion. There may be occasions when tactics of this kind are effective in stopping prevarication and encouraging concentration on the key issues. Running a bargaining session through the lunch period has already been mentioned. But there are several reasons for being very cautious about using this ploy in any more extreme form. It should be noted, too, that where all-night bargaining does occur, particularly in large-scale national negotiations, it is often because of logistics, not tactics. Senior employer and trade union representatives assemble from all over the country on a fixed date. Many will have very full diaries, and important appointments elsewhere on the following day. There is a mutual desire to complete the business on the appointed day and so avoid either disrupting the next day's arrangements or having to search for a possibly distant mutually convenient date for the resumption of the meeting if it has to be adjourned.

Among the other reasons for caution are:

There is no reason for thinking that managers are any less affected by exhaustion than trade union officials. Indeed, union officers may be far more used to protracted evening meetings than managers.

If the issues are at all complex, clear, cool thinking on both sides is desirable if the eventual agreement is to be soundly constructed. Tired negotiators, at 03 00 in a smoke-filled room, may find it easier to agree on a hastily written and consequently fudged form of words, than on a carefully drafted, unambiguous statement of settlement.

It is not possible to force anyone to stay at the negotiating table against their will. If the trade union side feels that it is being put at a disadvantage by the late hour, it is completely free to stop the meeting, ask for a date for its resumption, and go home.

If it is the management, rather than the trade union, who are concerned that the meeting may go on too long, it may be worth starting the meeting with a firm statement about the time it will have to finish. 'Two of us have important engagements this evening that we cannot pull out of, so we will have to finish by six at the latest.' If this line is taken, however, two points should be borne in mind. First, that adequate time is allowed for the meeting: most negotiations take longer than is initially expected. Second, that credibility will be undermined if, having announced an unalterable deadline, when the time comes it is ignored.

6　Negotiating tactics: II

The last chapter dealt with tactics which were concerned mainly with strengthening one's own position and weakening the other party's. In this chapter, the more collaborative or co-operative phase of negotiation is considered, when both parties work towards an eventual agreement. It needs to be emphasized that unless a willingness to reconsider the opening position exists – or develops during the discussions – a negotiation cannot be brought to an effective conclusion. This may seem too obvious a point to need emphasis. Unfortunately, the history of collective bargaining is littered with breakdowns which have occurred because one or other party, whether as a matter of strategy, stubbornness or stupidity, has at the end of the day been more concerned to maintain the rectitude of their original position than to resolve a dispute on the basis of an agreement which would have involved some compromise.

This is not to argue that all disputes can be resolved by negotiation, or that all trade union claims must be conceded at least in part. As was pointed out earlier in discussing the balance of power, occasions arise in which it may be judged possible and desirable to resolve matters unilaterally. One golden rule of negotiation is: if you don't have to negotiate, don't! This implies, though, that the very act of agreeing to negotiations is a signal to the other party that there is some possibility of compromise. For negotiations to be effective, that signal is best given in good faith.

Looking for links

An agreement, almost by definition, is an outcome in which both parties can see some advantage or benefit. There are some cases in which this may be very one-sided. A no-frills pay settlement, for example, may be agreed fairly grudgingly by the employer, with all the perceived advantage going to the trade union. Even here, though, the employer probably needs to keep wage rates in line with general trends, so the pay settlement is not really solely of benefit to the employees.

In many other instances, the benefits in an agreement will be more obviously mutual, and the more clearly this is seen to be the case the more readily will an agreement be reached. It is important, therefore, to look for links between the two initially different or opposing positions if progress is to be made towards agreement.

Such links are rarely direct or obvious. They usually lie behind the formally stated claims or cases, and often consist of some general principle with which both sides would concur, but which each is initially pursuing by a different route. A dispute used as an example in an earlier chapter illustrates this – the demand by a trade union for the dismissal of a supervisor for indulging in racial abuse. The opening positions are diametrically opposed. The union wants the supervisor sacked, the management does not. There is, however, a linking factor which eventually leads to a settlement. This link is that both parties share a concern for the avoidance in future of supervisory behaviour of this kind. A concentration on this common interest, rather than on the original difference, is the basis on which an agreement is eventually concluded.

Many other examples could be quoted, because there are many issues in which the underlying interests of employer and employees are the same – or at least similar. The avoidance of accidents at work, the maintenance of high morale, company prosperity and consequent job security are some of these common concerns. If the possible solution to an apparently narrow and detailed dispute can be shown to contribute to the achievement of such broader objectives, reaching agreement will be made much easier. So one way forward in the course of negotiating is to suggest: 'Perhaps we could put the detail on one side for a moment and have a look at any underlying principles which we might both think are important.'

Reading between the lines

Experienced negotiators are always wary of committing themselves too quickly and thus conceding more than may be really necessary. As the discussion moves into its later and more exploratory phase, it is consequently of critical importance to pick up even the faintest hint of a possible change of direction. The management may be pressing for agreement to abandon the concept of a fixed working week, and instead, introduce an annual working hours contract. After much discussion, the trade union leader may say: 'There is no possibility of my members going that far at this stage.' This is not a complete rejection of the proposal. There are two hints of possible progress. Put more directly, the trade union leader may be saying (by implication and in a negotiating 'code'): 'We might be willing to move towards an annual contract by stages, but not all at once immediately.' The two hints are, of course, 'going that far' – not that far, but perhaps some way: and 'at this stage' – meaning not immediately but perhaps later.

There is a whole glossary of these coded messages or signals. A few of the more common are:

'We could not agree to that this morning' – but if we are given some time to think about it and get advice from up the line we may be interested.

'We would find it very difficult to agree with that' – very difficult but not, perhaps, impossible.

'It wouldn't be our normal practice to do that' – but if the price is right we might be willing to consider it.

'You have put these proposals in a form which our members find unacceptable' – but if you were to reshape the package and provide a better explanation we might be able to make some progress.

'The one point which is totally unacceptable is x' – but w, y and z are worth talking about.

The general point, here, is to spot all the conditional statements and omissions, and then gently to follow these up to see if movement may be possible.

Signals of possible compromise may not only be verbal. It is also important to watch for changes of tone and expression. The trade union leader may have a quick word in the ear of the most influential shop steward; pay particular attention to what is next said. Or a note of hesitation or even embarrassment may creep in when a line is being pursued in which the spokesperson has no great confidence. The signalling of possible compromise may well coincide with a change of speaker. The leading speaker during the more combative first part of the negotiations may give way to a more conciliatory spokesperson. So an understanding of all the many nuances of interactive behaviour is of great assistance in reading between the lines and in identifying the go and no-go areas for constructive discussion. It is an aspect of negotiating skill which is dealt with in more detail in the next chapter.

Talking and listening

Perhaps the most common fault in negotiating is saying too much and listening too little. During the first, more combative phase, this is not so critical as later. That is the time for setting out one's own position and some repetition may be necessary to ensure complete understanding. It is also accepted practice during this phase to challenge and attempt to rebut the other side's arguments in a vigorous or forceful manner. All this may involve a fair amount of talking, with bouts of quick verbal exchanges and the registering, almost, of hits and misses in terms of debating points.

Once the collaborative phase is reached, and the search is on for common ground and acceptable compromise, far more priority should be given to listening. What is the other side really saying? What are the key concerns? What might the reaction be to a particular proposal? The answers will not be found by continuing to talk – only by perceptive listening. The question arises: what if the other side adopts the same tactic at the same time: will not the discussion just dry up? The solution is to switch from making statements to asking questions, and then listening carefully to the answers. Note, too, that a question from the other side can be answered with another question in order to facilitate this listening process. The trade union may ask: 'Is there any chance of you changing your minds on the issue of working hours?' The managerial reply might be: 'Could you explain why you seem to be giving this item such high priority?'

Helping the other party move

There are two very normal human characteristics which can inhibit the closing stages of a negotiation. First, there is a reluctance to be seen to change one's mind and to accept a worsening of one's original position. Secondly, there is a temptation to gloat over any retreat by one's opponent. The two points are obviously linked. Because negotiation inevitably has a competitive element, the outcomes tend to be seen in terms of winning or losing. Unfortunately, trade unions in particular tend publicly to claim 'victory' at the conclusion of negotiations in which, it will be said, major concessions have been wrung from unwilling employers. The less obvious the benefits, the more strident, sometimes, are the claims to have won.

There is a reason for this: it is not just bloody mindedness. Trade unions, unlike employers, are accountable to very large electorates. The majority of members do not understand the rituals, dynamics and power realities of the negotiating process. They may well be wholly convinced that their union's formal claim is fully justified or, indeed, that it represents the bare minimum of what is their due. There follows a long and difficult negotiation in which it becomes patently obvious to the union's negotiators that their initial claim must be significantly modified to achieve a settlement. Their thanks for skilful bargaining in which such modification is kept to the minimum will probably be accusations of having 'sold the membership down the river', unless they are able to explain why the original claim was, in practice, unobtainable. One way of doing this is to dramatize the battle with the employers, and so to present the outcome using the battlefield metaphors of victory for us, and defeat for them. If the outcome is so poor that this will not wash, then there is always the fallback cliché of 'We may have lost the battle but we will still win the war.'

There are three lessons here for management. One is that it pays to develop a thick skin regarding this kind of ritualized union posturing. Agreements will not easily be reached if there is too much concern, either about the implication of 'defeat' in making concessions, or about the union's possible exaggeration of its 'victory'. Secondly, it does not pay to indulge in similar posturing. When the union makes a concession it may be tempting to score a point by making a remark about back-tracking or the unreality of their original claim. In one negotiation, any subsequent union movement was lost when, in response to the union's first concession, the management leader commented impatiently: 'We could have saved a lot of time if you had agreed to that in the first place instead of wasting two hours defending the indefensible!'

The third, and more important point leads on from this. It is worthwhile doing everything possible to make it easy for the other party to move. This implies the very opposite of gloating over their retreat: it means helping them to see the benefits to them, not to you, of the concessions you want them to make. Take the subject of cashless pay. The advantage to the employer is mainly financial, ie the payroll costs less to administer. That is not the factor, though, which will sell the idea to a somewhat reluctant negotiating team of manual workers' shop stewards. They will need to understand the benefits to them, not the employer, and it is those benefits which will need emphasis in the bargaining session.

A wage negotiation may result in a much lower settlement than the union initially expected. To clinch this agreement, management as well as the union's negotiators, need to think about how the union might make the best of it. 'Would it help,' the management might ask, 'if we issued a statement saying that the settlement at this level will help to protect the 500 jobs in our northern plant?'

Whatever the particular details may be, the principle to follow is that of helping the other party identify the advantages to them, not of emphasizing the benefits to oneself.

The use of humour

Observe the behaviour when they first meet of two negotiating teams, or just two negotiators, who already know each other. Before starting serious discussions, there is almost always a short period of good-natured joshing or banter. 'Open the windows, George has brought his fumigator!' might be the personnel manager's comment about the principal union negotiator's famous pipe. Or the union convenor might ask for a newspaper to sit on. 'That's alright', says the manager, 'you're not that grubby!' 'It's not that', says the convenor, delighted that the manager has walked into the trap, 'I just don't want to catch anything!'

This type of rough and ready humour serves two purposes. First, it helps to reduce the inevitable underlying tension. Secondly, it helps to establish a shared, rather than confrontational relationship. This bonding is not particularly strong. It will quickly break down when serious differences of view occur which each party defends with passion. Nevertheless, most negotiations make better progress if the initial, sometimes rather nervous *bonhomie* is reinforced from time to time during the discussions with a well-chosen and well-timed light-hearted and good-humoured remark.

This is not a matter of telling jokes. It involves spotting the occasional absurdity or mistake, particularly when this emanates from one's own team, and drawing attention to its funny side. It does not call for great wit; the too-clever comment may well be perceived as sarcasm rather than humour. It must not, therefore, be based on such things as a shop steward's or manager's unwitting mispronunciation of some technical or managerial jargon. It must imply that we are all in this together, we are all human and fallible, and let's all keep a sense of proportion. It is, unfortunately, impossible to define in terms of any definitive formula.

Avoiding loss of face

The battle ethos in industrial relations, and the normal reluctance to change one's position, reinforce the fear of losing face – the feeling of personal failure, publicly exposed. This is a powerful influence on negotiating behaviour because it has two dimensions.

First, any individual member of a negotiating team may hesitate to be the first to suggest a modification of position for fear of being thought 'wet' by his or her own side. Teams tend to reinforce their internal optimism about 'winning', and can be very reluctant to examine the weaknesses in their positions. The first team member to say: 'I don't think we can sustain our original position: I think we will have to make a concession here', may well be subjected initially to attack by the rest of the team for letting the side down.

Secondly, there is the fear of losing influence or status in the eyes of the other party. 'We can't concede on that point: the trade union will think we've gone soft.'

It can be seen, then, that the fear of losing face can inhibit the achievement of constructive compromise both within either side, and between the two sides.

To avoid this factor impeding progress demands sensitivity and skill in the way in which changes or concessions are proposed and responded to. The primary point is to emphasize the positive and favourable elements of changes in position, rather than too obviously dwelling on their negative aspects. This is of particular importance when responding to movement from the other side. The trade union may indicate, somewhat tentatively and perhaps with some underlying embarrassment about being thought to be unusually conciliatory, that it might be prepared to trade off its claim for a shorter working week against an improvement in annual leave. If the management wants to encourage this movement, then the response it should not make is: 'That's a bit of a climb-down, isn't it!' Instead of belittling the trade union's standing in this way, positive encouragement is needed, perhaps along these lines: 'That's a very interesting and responsible suggestion: I am sure it gives us both a basis for making progress.' Instead of losing face by being considered weak, the union is flattered by being congratulated for wisdom and responsibility.

There is a related point. Loss of face, and consequent adverse reaction, occurs when either party gets trapped into a position from which the only escape appears to be an obvious and humiliating retreat. The danger then is that instead of accepting such humiliation, negotiations will be broken off and there will be a resort to direct confrontation. It pays, therefore, to allow the other party some form of back-door escape route – some concession or explanation, however minor in substance – which will allow them to point to some off-setting advantage and so avoid the degradation of defeat. It follows that unless one is wholly and justifiably confident of one's own position, it is also sensible to keep one's own back-door open to provide for the possibility of a dignified withdrawal. The loss of managerial credibility and face caused by making a succession of 'final offers' has been referred to earlier.

Periodic summaries

As the negotiation moves through the more discursive and exploratory phase in which each side is feeling its way towards a possible agreement, it is easy to lose track of progress, and for an argument on some late point to result in the loss of tentative agreement reached at an earlier stage in the discussion.

It is consequently helpful to pause from time to time to summarize the progress which has been made. The management leader might say: 'Before we move on to talk about overtime premia, we might all find it helpful to run over where we have got to on working time. As I understand it, your position is that your current priority is annual leave and we are prepared to go along with this. We have agreed, I think, that the precise extent of any improvement will need to be worked out when we come to costing the full package, but we have already said that we are willing to bring the manuals' entitlement in line with basic grade clericals. Is everyone happy with that summary? If so, we'll just make a quick note of it so that we needn't waste time later trying to remember what we agreed.'

This may, of course, reveal that the two sides have different understandings about the position which has been reached. That may be frustrating, but it is still better to sort this out in stages, than to reach the end of a lengthy and complex negotiation, only to find that there are major differences of view as to what has been agreed in the course of the discussions.

Using hypothetical suggestions

The later phase of negotiation has been described as exploratory. Reference has also been made to the reluctance of experienced negotiators to show their hands too quickly. How, then, can any real progress be made? One very useful and widely used tactic is to put forward ideas on a hypothetical and no-commitment basis.

A union claim for higher overtime premia may be under discussion. The management may have it in mind to cut the overtime bill by putting in a Saturday morning shift, staffed by part-timers on plain time rates. But they may not wish to commit themselves to this until they have sounded out union reaction. They realize, too, that some improvement in overtime premia may well be the price for agreement about the Saturday shift but they do not want to be trapped into offering anything specific in advance of a firm acceptance by the union of the new shift arrangement. One way of leading into a discussion on this topic would be to raise it hypothetically. The management leader might say: 'We fully understand your views about the current levels of overtime premia, but I know that you realize we have to look at the costs involved very carefully. Might there be some way of going towards you on premia without pushing our unit costs up too much? Suppose, for sake of argument, that we found some way of dealing with the Saturday morning problem as a form of normal shift working.' The phrase 'for sake of argument' shows that at this point no firm proposal is being made. On the other hand there is the hint of a possible deal – higher premia for weekday overtime against a cut in Saturday morning payments. Note, too, that at this early point no figures have been mentioned.

An approach of this kind meets the criteria of several of the preceding paragraphs. No loss of face will be involved either in the trade union expressing guarded interest or in the management changing or even abandoning the idea. It has got a new idea onto the table without creating a commitment either on the management to defend it, or the union to oppose it. It will probably open the door to further discussion in which, by a process of probing, questioning and explanation, an increasingly specific set of proposals can emerge for potential agreement.

Introductory phrases, in addition to 'for the sake of argument' might be:

'Without commitment at this stage, what might be your response to a proposal that . . .'

'Suppose we thought of doing something along these lines – how might you react? . . .'

'We had thought at one stage that we might suggest x, but perhaps this is not quite what you had in mind?'

'Have you ever thought about y as an alternative? It is something we might find it possible to consider.'

Constructive compromise

Demonstrating to one's own side, as well as to the other party, that a proposed concession has positive as well as negative elements, is one aspect of treating compromise as constructive. Put this way it may, however, smack of window-dressing or the claiming of advantage for the sake of presentation, even when the substance does not merit so optimistic a view.

The achievement of genuinely constructive compromise goes deeper, and in many ways pulls together most of the separate points which have already been discussed. If useful conditions are tied to any concessions, if common interests have been identified and reinforced, if both parties have retained their mutual respect and self regard, and if both can claim some benefit from the outcome of their discussions, it is probable that their agreement is constructive in both reality and appearance.

The detailed points which have already been discussed do not need repetition here. What is worth emphasizing is the value, throughout a negotiation, of a continual search for the positive. How can this or that proposal be used to achieve a wider benefit than might first seem possible? Can a new condition be introduced to offset the disadvantages of a pending concession? Would a change of emphasis or priority secure long term advantage against short term loss? Questions of this kind should be continuously in mind.

In thinking of longer term benefits, it is also important to look well beyond the subject matter of the particular negotiation. Can the negotiation be conducted in a way which will improve the future general relationship between management and trade union? Will a tactical retreat on a narrow issue this week provide a better basis for success on a much more important matter which is due to be discussed next week? Can a fairly minor withdrawal by the union, or an equally small advance in the management position, be used as a precedent at a later stage for further strengthening of managerial power or influence?

It is on questions of this kind that thought needs to be concentrated, rather than wasting mental energy agonizing over whether or not every minor compromise might be seen as weakness.

'Fudge'

At the end of a difficult and complicated negotiation, when it transpires that there are still some unresolved points which are delaying agreement on what are perceived as the major issues, it is possible to reach a conclusion by forms of words which gloss over the disputed matters – in other words, the awkward points are fudged.

For example, there may be a negotiation about new working practices in an office following the introduction of new technology. Agreement has been reached about the main allocations of work between the various jobs, and on some regrading. The trade union has, however, expressed concern about cramped working conditions and sought agreement, which the management has felt unable to concede, to 90 square feet of office space being allocated to each worker. Rather than have this point hold up the whole agreement, both sides agree a statement that: 'In determining the working layout of the office, management will, among other factors, have regard to the union's view that the layout, as originally proposed, was not wholly adequate in terms of floor space per employee.' What does this mean in practice? What is the implication of phrases such as 'have regard to', and 'among other factors'. No-one really knows, they are just forms of words which, precisely because of their vagueness or ambiguity, each side can interpret in its own way.

If the fudged issue really is of very minor importance, then perhaps the fudge is justifiable. The possibility of this causing a slight difficulty at a later stage may be an acceptable price to pay for an otherwise major and satisfactory settlement.

In many instances, however, such failure to face and settle points of difference demonstrates a weakness in negotiating tactics, and too often merely defers a dispute about a matter which has, sooner or later, to be dealt with head on. It is a particular weakness of professional negotiators in national or industry-wide bargaining who are not faced directly with the realities of interpreting and applying their agreements at local level. If the negotiators are too remote from the practical application of their agreements, they may tend to see the conclusion of an agreement – the signing of the piece of paper – as an end in itself. It is no coincidence that at national level, concern for 'a form of words' to settle a dispute is often all but obsessive. The phrase has become part of the ritual. The result is sometimes form at national level which is acceptable, but content at local level which is unintelligible. When that occurs, the negotiators have lost sight of the fact that although signing an agreement is the end of that negotiation, it is also the beginning of a probably longer period of implementation. This requires clarity, not fudge.

Closing the deal

Commercial negotiators place great importance on the tactics and psychology of closing the deal. It also figures particularly strongly in sales training – judging when the time has come to get the customer to sign the order form.

In industrial relations bargaining, many of the more manipulative selling techniques are too crude to be effective. It is nevertheless of great importance to judge when the time has come during negotiation to bring the concession-making and mutual exploration of possibilities to a close, to indicate that one can go no further, and to achieve the agreement of the other side to the position which has then been reached.

Two factors are critically important – timing, and the credibility of the final offer.

Timing is important because the mood, or emotional atmosphere, of a bargaining meeting fluctuates between 'highs' of *bonhomie* and co-operation, and 'lows' of disagreements and even anger. It is fairly obvious that the right time to suggest that agreement is possible is during a high.

Credibility is important on both sides. There will come a point beyond which one or other side will genuinely be unable or determined not to move. They will say so. Will they be believed by the other side? There is a real problem if one or other side cannot establish credibility for such statements. To a large extent this will depend on previous experience. The management which has a record of prevarication and back-tracking will find it very difficult to persuade the trade union that the end of the road has really been reached.

Within the context of a meeting, statements about finality can be reinforced by the tone of voice, by a change of style from a discursive mode to one of short, crisp statements, and by gestures, such as putting all one's papers together and reaching for one's briefcase.

Other aids to effecting a close are:

Keeping one concession in reserve to be used to break any possible final deadlock

Tying the proposed agreement to some additional future benefit: 'If we settle on this package now, the company will make a commitment to re-open the question of the working week in next year's pay negotiation.'

Explaining fully the reasons why no further movement is possible, perhaps by bringing in the sales director to provide a graphic account of the implications of any further price rises

Reiterating and emphasizing the benefits of the proposed deal

Pointing up the adverse consequences of a breakdown in negotiation.

Ensuring full understanding

For an agreement to be effective in the full sense of the word, it is essential, before the meeting closes and the participants disperse, to ensure that what has been agreed is quite clear to all concerned. The time to clear up any misunderstandings about this is before negotiations close, not afterwards.

So if the trade union leader does not suggest it, the management leader should say something along these lines: 'I think we have now dealt with all the issues and reached agreement on what we are going to do. I think it would be helpful if we summarized the whole thing. So my understanding is that what we have agreed is this: . . .' going on to list each point and its outcome.

If intermediate summaries have been used, as was suggested earlier in this chapter, this final summary should be relatively easy. If not, it is as well to be prepared for at least a few points to be revealed on which some further joint clarification is necessary.

Ending on a high note

Effective implementation of most agreements requires a degree of support and commitment by both management and trade union. With a view to future relationships it is also useful to reinforce the union's willingness to agree to concessions and compromise.

For both these reasons, and to maintain managerial morale, the satisfactory conclusion of a difficult negotiation can legitimately be made the subject of mutual congratulations and, perhaps, a modest celebration.

The line is: 'Well, that wasn't easy for either side, and we had some very sticky moments, but in the end we all showed that we have the ability and willingness to work together to solve our own problems. Neither of us has got all we wanted, but we've both got something out of our final agreement and this augurs well for our future dealings. Now let's all adjourn to the local hostelry for a well-earned drink!'

Of course, cynical, case-hardened, professional negotiators will recognize this as part of the ritual. But as we have seen, ritual has its functional value, and in this case its purpose is to reduce the tensions and sometimes bitterness of argument as quickly as possible, to generate a sense of achievement instead of defeat, and to lay the basis for the next effective negotiation.

Producing written confirmation

Even when a thorough verbal summing up has occurred, it is essential to get the agreement into written form as soon as possible. Managers and employees not involved in the negotiations, to say nothing of the media, are going to ask the participants immediately about what has been agreed. By the time a verbal version has been passed on several times it will be distorted, incomplete or inaccurate. The only remedy is the rapid and extensive issue of a definitive written version.

This is so important that the management and trade union leaders – or the personnel manager with a relevant trade union official – may well need to stay together after the other participants disperse in order to draft an agreed document. Alternatively, the management representative may write a draft the next day, and clear it with the appropriate union official on the phone or at a quick meeting.

Even in small-scale and relatively informal negotiations, the quick, written confirmation is valuable. For example, a production manager has a meeting with the senior shop steward to deal with a union complaint about the operation of a quality bonus. They agree a minor change in the procedure. The manager would be well-advised to produce a memo to the steward saying: 'I am writing to confirm the outcome of our useful discussion this morning. You queried the method of calculating the scrap rate when sub-standard materials were discovered. I agreed that in future, rejects caused by sub-standard materials would be discounted in the week in which they occurred instead of, as now, one week in arrears.'

It may be noted that in the preceding examples, the agreement is written, or at least drafted initially, by management. There is an undoubted advantage in this task being undertaken by the management side. This is not a matter of introducing distortions, or of sliding into the agreement points which were not actually agreed. To go that far would be to risk justifiable criticism for deceit. Nevertheless, the party which actually writes down the agreement does have the advantage of choosing the words, sequence and even layout which that party considers is the clearest and most satisfactory exposition from its point of view. If there is no agreed or customary practice on this point it is as well for management to volunteer to produce the document, or just to act on the assumption that this is obviously their task. So the management leader might conclude by saying: 'We ought to get this down on paper as quickly as possible, so we will produce a draft tomorrow morning and check it through with you on the phone.'

7   Negotiating abilities

Some people are better negotiators than others. Like most human activities, differences in negotiating ability result, at least in part, from differences in individual personality and aptitudes. Some writers have described the effective negotiator almost entirely in terms of these personal characteristics. Leigh,[1] for example, suggests that in addition to a knowledge of the subject under negotiation, the good bargainer needs:

- A quick mind
- Unlimited patience
- An ability to conceal opinions and facts without lying
- Capacity to inspire trust in others
- To be self-effacing yet assertive at key moments
- An ability to see the wood for the trees.

There is no doubt that the possession of such qualities goes a long way towards making an effective negotiator. The trouble is that very few managers, or for that matter trade union officials, could claim to meet all these criteria, and to the extent that they are basic personality traits it is not possible to acquire them by any simple process of reading or training.

Yet it is possible to improve one's negotiating abilities, and this chapter examines the factors lying behind effective negotiation, and the role that training can play in achieving such improvement. There are three broad factors involved, each with several elements:

Knowledge: of industrial relations and collective bargaining principles
of the specific industrial relations context
of the particular negotiation
of the subject matter under negotiation.

Skill: analytical skill
             social or interactive skills
             communicating skill.

Attitude: towards collective bargaining generally
             towards the specifics of each negotiation
             towards one's own role.

Each of these elements is now considered in more detail, and the chapter concludes with a section on training for negotiation.

Knowledge of principles

It is difficult for any manager to feel at ease or confident in negotiations with trade unions without an understanding of the wider industrial relations context in which these negotiations occur. Even in the very informal situation of a supervisor discussing a shop floor complaint with a single shop steward, a lack of knowledge about the constitutional role and powers of a steward will weaken the supervisor's position.

In the more formal negotiating arenas of company or national negotiations, this need for a sound knowledge of basic industrial relations and collective bargaining principles becomes more marked. There are three main aspects to this:

1   *The nature of trade unions as institutions,* with particular reference to the way authority and responsibility are distributed. A common managerial failing is to think of a trade union as having the same hierarchy of authority as a company, in which authority flows from the top down. In trade unions, authority and power ultimately lie at the bottom with the membership: the complete inverse of the company or managerial model. It is also important for the manager to understand the differing roles and powers of lay union officials – the elected shop stewards – and full-time union officers who are, in effect, the unions' own employees. Full-time officers often act as unions' leading negotiators, but this does not imply that they have the authority to conclude agreements. They normally have to refer back, either to a shop stewards' committee

or to the membership at large by ballot or mass meeting, to get authority actually to conclude a deal.

2 *The nature of the collective bargaining process,* including all the rituals and conventions which have been described in the preceding chapters. Inexperienced managerial negotiators often find these conventions irksome, and question their logicality. 'What is the point of this interminable haggling? Why don't we just tell the union what our position is and then stick to it – take it or leave it.' To grasp just the elementary point that to justify their existence to their members, trade union representatives need to be seen to have had to work hard to achieve a settlement, may help such a manager come to terms with the realities of negotiation.

3 *The main legal factors* which may impinge on collective bargaining. These are dealt with in the next chapter, but the three key points are the absence in the UK of legally binding agreements, the statutory requirements regarding ballots for industrial action, and the legal constraints on secondary or sympathetic industrial action.

Knowledge of the specific context

In addition to a good working knowledge of the general industrial relations and collective bargaining scene, negotiators need a much more detailed understanding of how this operates in their own particular organization and industry. The main points to check are:

What trade unions are involved and how are they organized?

Starting at local level, what are the union branches? Are they based on the organization and its workplaces, or do they cover geographical areas which include other employers?

What are the unions' district and/or regional groupings, and how are the local branches linked to them?

What is the chain of communication and authority from branch to district to region to national level? What authority does the union rule book prescribe at each level to conclude agreements, vary nationally or regionally negotiated conditions of service, approve or initiate industrial action?

How are officials and officers elected and/or appointed, and what are their roles and powers?

Are any union elections pending at the time of the negotiations?

What are the organization's own domestic agreements and procedures regarding the resolution of disputes, joint consultative arrangements and negotiating practices?

What are the limits on managerial authority at the various levels in the hierarchy so far as changes in conditions of service, working conditions, working practices and disciplinary action are concerned? Which managers have what roles in the resolution of disputes and in collective bargaining? Does the personnel or industrial relations manager have an executive or advisory function in this respect?

What are the limits, if any, on the organization's authority to negotiate and agree changes in pay and conditions of service? Are some issues a matter for regional, industrial or national settlement? If the organization is one establishment or subsidiary within a larger group, do some issues (and if so which) have to be referred to head office?

Who are the personalities involved on the union side? Who are the hard men, the realists, the mavericks, the conciliators, the trustworthy, the manipulators? Which have the greatest influence on the shop floor? How do the various individuals relate to each other? Who are the rivals? What are the cliques?

This long list of questions is not exhaustive, but what it illustrates is the very wide range of information about the local context of negotiation which ought to be part of every negotiator's kit. Experience indicates that far too many managers walk into negotiations with a wholly inadequate knowledge of the procedures, personalities and dynamics of their local industrial relations arena. In consequence, they can be caught out by the union side for departing from formal precedents, be uncertain as to how far they can go in making concessions, fall foul of their own senior management for being either too cautious or too innovative, fail to understand where real power and influence lies on the union side and, in general, undermine their own bargaining position by giving the union the impression of a lack of understanding, confidence and professionalism.

On the other hand, a thorough understanding of the local scene and its links with regional and national systems can go a long way towards compensating for some lack of the personal skills listed at the beginning of this chapter.

Knowledge of the subject matter

It must be obvious that negotiators, however otherwise skilled and well-informed, cannot perform well in negotiation unless they have all relevant information about the issue under discussion at their finger tips.

In one bargaining session, a managing director waxed eloquent for 10 minutes on why it was impossible to concede that part of a package claim which sought two extra days off at Christmas. 'If it was a matter simply for this company,' he said (not wholly sincerely), 'I would be sympathetic; but as you know, we have always kept to the national industrial agreement on leave and I can't depart from that now.' The trade union leader took a document out of his briefcase. 'You seem to have forgotten', he said, 'that in 1982 the national agreement was amended to include a sentence which states that the annual leave provisions exclude any supplementary leave which companies may grant at Christmas on a local basis. So you haven't got a problem and we'll accept your offer of two extra days!'

Being caught out in this way undermines credibility in the eyes of the other side, and saps a manager's self-confidence. So the subject matter should always be thoroughly researched, including current factors and any history of previous negotiations and precedents.

It is not always possible to remember or have available every last detail which may arise in the course of negotiation. There are two ways of dealing with this. First, never make an assertion about a fact which is capable of being checked, unless you are absolutely certain it is correct. Secondly, if a matter is raised by the trade union on which you are uncertain of the facts, do not accept the union's assertions – ask to see chapter and verse, or call an adjournment to check the position. There is far more credibility to be gained from saying: 'I'm not sure of the facts on that – let's have a short adjournment while I look it up on the file:' than there is in bluffing the matter out, only to be proved wrong.

Analytical skills

In many negotiations the issues may be complex with many permutations of possible concessions and compromise. There will often also be a hidden agenda on both sides – unspoken objectives about, for example, changes in power or influence. If an effective negotiating plan is to be evolved, then the same type of analysis will be needed as in any other type of business problem.

In other words, the points to identify are:

What is the central issue? What are the more peripheral matters?

What is the central objective? What are the supplementary aims?

What are the main barriers to achieving the objective? What are the factors which will assist?

What alternative approaches are there, and what are their strengths and weaknesses? Which is the best?

What data or arguments will best serve the chosen approach and aims?

What contingency action should be planned?

This initial analysis should also include the perceived strong and weak points in the other side's position, not just in terms of their actual claim or case, but also in regard to their personalities, politics (with a small p) and power structures.

The analytical skills involved are similar to those of the management consultant or business analyst, or in the writing of a complex report in which the key elements of a situation are identified, followed by the pros and cons of alternative actions, leading to a preferred and costed solution. Given that not all managers can combine these skills with all the others required in effective negotiation, there is much to be said for forming a small negotiating team so that collective wisdom can be applied and different aspects of the whole process allocated to individuals to match the particular and different talents of each.

Social and interactive skills

The negotiating meeting itself involves very intense verbal, personal and social interaction. This includes both individual and group elements: individual, in the sense of person-to-person exchanges and a variety of personal roles; group, to the extent that each side has a collective style and set of attitudes of its own. The good negotiator has an either intuitive or trained ability to sense out the changing mood and concerns of individuals and groups, and to adopt the appropriate behaviour to influence these dynamics. This book cannot go into the whole psychological and sociological basis of individual and group behaviour. What can be suggested here are some aspects of negotiation behaviour on which it is fairly safe to generalize and which either aid or impede effective negotiation.

Negative behaviour, or behaviour which tends to generate unco-operative reaction, is often highly personal in its psychological basis. That is, the person involved behaves in a way which projects, protects or promotes their own concept of the sort of person they are, and is concerned more with the preservation or enhancement of their own dignity or self-regard, than with making constructive progress on the matter in hand. They may not be fully conscious that they are behaving in this way, but that is how their behaviour appears to other people. Particular points to avoid, therefore, are:

An excessive or inappropriate use of the personal pronoun. Only an owner-manager of a business should say: 'I cannot afford to offer more than six per cent,' or: 'I can go as far as one extra day's leave but that is my outside limit.' For managers who are, in reality, negotiating not on their own behalf but as company representatives, the personalization of views in this way is unwise. The type of reaction it generates, spoken or unspoken, is: 'Who does he think he is – it's not his money!'

A related fault: criticizing the other side personally, instead of commenting on their arguments. Thus the response to a trade union complaint about alleged victimization by a supervisor might be: 'I cannot understand how you can possibly believe what you have just said.' This is nearly as direct as saying: 'I think you are a fool or a liar!' Anyone with an ounce of self-respect would react strongly to such an inference – regardless of the underlying facts. A more constructive response would be: 'That's a serious and disturbing statement which needs more explanation.' The impersonal comment avoids the risk of the real issue being lost in an emotional reaction to what might be perceived as a personal attack.

Point-scoring, just for the pleasure of doing so. Anyone who enjoys an argument and considers themselves fairly quick-witted is in danger of falling into this trap. Here is one such managerial contribution to a pay negotiation. The rather ponderous trade union leader has just been expounding on the importance of improving the lot of the lower graded staff. The management spokesperson interrupts: 'You realize you have just defeated one of your own arguments. This morning you told us of your wish to see an improvement in differentials. It's a statistical impossibility to do this and improve the relative position of the lower paid. So do we forget this morning and look at the latter, or drop the low pay argument and go back to differentials – because you can't have both!' This comment may be wholly sound in logic, but it has been expressed in a manner guaranteed to raise the union's hackles. A better response would be: 'This morning you drew attention to differentials. This afternoon you have asked us to consider the lower paid. We are not quite clear how these two points can both be dealt with in the same pay settlement. Perhaps you can help us with a more detailed explanation.' Note that this less 'clever' or aggressive response is not in reality weaker than the point-scoring reply. By inviting further explanation it is probable the union speaker will either get even further into the mire, and so weaken the case, or will see the illogicality of the case for himself and then modify the claim. Point-scoring, or sarcasm which is worse, will strengthen rather than weaken the other side's resolve.

Allocating fault or blame. A disciplinary or accident enquiry needs to identify failings and determine who was responsible. In very few negotiations is such an approach desirable. Negotiations are about the future. If the discussion tends to fall into arguments about who did or said what at some earlier date, the temptation to pursue this for the sake of being proved right should be resisted. The right line generally is: 'Don't let's waste time on a post-mortem: we agree that something went wrong, but let's spend our time on discussing how to prevent it happening again.'

Frequently interrupting. The style of some speakers is somewhat turgid. Inexperienced managers or lay officials may also have difficulty in presenting a clear, concise and coherently argued case. There is consequently a strong temptation to interrupt – either to clarify the point at issue or to make a swift riposte. This is a temptation to be resisted. It is very important that the speakers should feel that they have been able to say everything they consider necessary.

Positive negotiating behaviour is to a large extent the opposite of what has just been described, though there are some additional aspects. The underlying theme in terms of interactive skills is to create an atmosphere in which the other side will feel that their concessions and agreements are positive, clever and reasonable, rather than being evidence of weakness or defeat. The main points are:

Listening and questioning. Having the patience to let the other side talk itself out has already been referred to. Of equal importance is the use of questions, rather than statements, to draw out flaws in the other side's case and to probe proposals.

Summarizing. This has also been referred to in the previous chapter.

Looking for and recognizing signals. One of the main interactive skills is the ability to sense the changing moods and attitudes of individuals and groups. It is of particular importance in negotiating, where the timing of reaching a conclusion (knowing when to stop and when to close the deal) is of the essence. Signals are by no means only verbal. Obviously one needs to listen to the words, but it is also necessary to consider the tone of voice, facial expressions, and 'body language'. If the other side begins to sit back with folded arms, for example, this may be a sign of an adverse reaction. Watch, too, for signs of group cohesion or disintegration. Does one person pull slightly away from the speaker in the next seat? When the leader is speaking, do the other members of that side look at him or her with supportive gestures (eg nodding vigorously) or do they look at the table or the ceiling, avoiding eye contact with the other side. The latter may well indicate that they think their spokesperson has gone too far.

Using eye contact. In normal conversation, frequent eye contact is of major importance in determining who speaks when, and indicating which parts of the discussion are of most interest to each participant. Attention can be gained and held by looking the person being addressed straight in the eye. On the other hand, if one wants to make a long statement without interruption, it may help if all eye contact is avoided. The statement will, though, come across as rather impersonal. To hold the whole of the other side's attention, without inviting eye-generated interruption, it is better to sweep one's eye contact to and fro across all the faces on the other side of the table, while leaning forward, talking in an animated fashion, and perhaps reinforcing key points by gestures (eg stabbing a pencil at one's papers).

Following negatives with positives. It is conducive to a co-operative atmosphere to conclude any important statement whenever possible on a positive rather than negative note. There is a tendency in discussion for each party to respond more to the closing words of the other party's last statement than to what may be a more important point made earlier in that statement. A negative end to a statement is therefore likely to generate a negative response. So do not say: 'We are interested in your proposals about re-defining entitlements to car allowances, but we are not willing to raise the mileage payments.' Instead, reverse the order of the two points: 'Raising the mileage payments is a problem, but we are interested in the redefinition of entitlement.'

Communicating skills

The ability to communicate effectively is, of course, part of the wider arena of interactive skills. In that context it includes, as has been discussed above, both verbal and non-verbal elements.

But the negotiating process as a whole is not limited to verbal and direct interpersonal interaction. It may include exchanges of correspondence, and should always include the written confirmation of actual agreements. In both spoken and written modes, the importance of clarity of meaning and expression merits emphasis. Here we consider that aspect of communication which is concerned with the use and choice of words.

Two main, common failings can be identified; first, a tendency to use unnecessarily formal, stilted language (often salted with managerial jargon); secondly, a tendency to be too indirect in relaying bad news.

Managers should remember that in communicating with trade unionists they are not dealing with managerial colleagues, and they should not, therefore, assume the same level of understanding of business jargon. Even when writing to a full-time union officer, who may well be the equal of any manager in such understanding, it needs to be kept in mind that the letter may be shown to shop stewards or employees at large. What to the manager and the union's professional negotiator may be a conventional business communication, may seem to the shop floor to be cold, devious and even offensive. One manager, explaining why a pay rise was all but impossible, said: 'What we must ask you to accept is that over the past year the company has enjoyed a negative rate of growth in both sales volumes and operating margins: you can see the effect by looking at the adverse change in our p/e ratio.' Said one shop steward to another: 'What the hell's he on about?' How much better it would have been to have said: 'During the past year our sales have fallen, we are not making a profit, and our share price is now so low that we risk being taken over.'

Wrapping up unpalatable news is a very natural thing to do, but it can cause serious problems. If a claim cannot be conceded, if no further compromise is possible, if a factory has to close, if a management decision is going to be imposed – say so clearly; the issue should not be fudged. In the long term, there is more credibility to be gained by acquiring a reputation for saying 'no' in an effective and acceptable manner, than from making endless concessions or from clouding unpleasant issues. In turning down a claim for additional pay for working in inclement weather, a manager once said: 'This claim poses difficulties. Not that we haven't examined it carefully and, indeed, some of my colleagues have expressed a good deal of sympathy – were it not for the fact that it is not something our competitors do and we are very reluctant to step out of line. There is also the question of cost, which we haven't been able to estimate accurately in the absence of detailed weather records, though I'm sure you understand the difficulty. So you can see our problem.' The convenor of the shop stewards replied: 'You told us this morning that you would give us a decision on this point: we're not interested to hear about your problems. Are you saying yes or no?' There is no doubt that the majority of union negotiators prefer and accept without rancour a firm, unemotional 'no' when this has to be the message – provided that the management is prepared to give an explanation.

Attitudes

Any person's ability to exercise skills effectively in any situation is influenced by their attitude towards that situation. In a negotiating context, a manager, however skilled, who harbours a strong feeling of resentment about having to spend time arguing with trade union officials, is less likely to negotiate effectively than a colleague who accepts, attitudinally, that the negotiation is necessary and important.

Attitudes are important in three respects – to the employer/trade union relationship generally; to the personalities involved in the particular negotiation; and to the topic under discussion.

Managers who hold a deeply rooted view that trade unions are a menace to society and the economy are not likely to make very effective negotiators. They may be the best choice to manage a planned confrontation, or to implement a strategy designed primarily to undermine union power and influence regardless of the subject matter of negotiations, but that is not the topic of this book.

Managers working in organizations in which trade unions are well-established and in which the employer/trade union relationship is necessarily close and frequent, must come to terms with that reality if they are to avoid the danger of their negotiating ability being undermined by outbursts of resentful expression or behaviour when frustrating episodes occur in the course of the bargaining process.

Strong personal like or dislike of personalities on the other side of the negotiating table can also distort bargaining behaviour. The urge to score points is particularly strong when the person opposite is disliked. The reluctance to disappoint a well-liked individual needs also to be watched. The safeguard in both cases is to concentrate on the issues, not the personalities.

Belief in one's own case is also important. It is very difficult to hold convincingly to a particular position or line of argument if at heart it is felt to be illogical or unfair. This is something to be considered in the pre-negotiation planning phase. 'Is our case really tenable? Is our objective realistically achievable?' These are the questions to answer, and answer honestly, before embarking on negotiation in which, if the realities of the position have not been fully faced, a lack of belief or commitment in the management case will soon begin to appear.

Training in negotiation

Although natural aptitudes and skills vary, and although the best negotiators are probably those with the highest level of innate ability, the negotiating ability of most managers can be improved by various forms of training.

The four main subject areas for such training are:

1   *The principles and practice of collective bargaining.* This is mainly a knowledge-based topic, covering the general background of the nature of trade unions, negotiating procedures and related general and local systems and practices as discussed earlier in this chapter. Training can include attendance at external and internal courses and seminars, together with planned reading.

2   *Interactive skills.* The ability to perform effectively in both individual and group situations can be improved by training activities which provide managers with an insight into the nature of their personalities and the impact of their behaviour on other people. There is a variety of relevant training techniques. They include sensitivity or T-group training, the use of psychometric tests to analyse personality traits, questionnaires or exercises to identify managerial style.

3   *Negotiating behaviour.* This is a more specific area of training covering the practical conduct of negotiations. There are two main training methods apart from the reading of relevant textbooks. Role-playing is used extensively by trainers who specialize in this subject as, of all training techniques, it comes closest to simulating the real thing. It is normal to use video recordings of the role play

to provide a clearer insight into how each person projects and reacts. It must be realized, though, that no role play can replicate all the pressures and dynamics of an actual negotiation. There is tendency, too, for inexperienced participants to act in a role play in accordance with preconceived stereotypes of, for example, the militant shop steward.

Another training method is coached observation. The manager under training sits in on actual negotiations and is asked to observe and analyse each side's performance. This analysis is then discussed with one of the experienced management negotiators, often the personnel manager. This is a very effective training method but it is very manager-intensive as it can normally be arranged for only one trainee at a time.

4 *Communication skills.* Improving a manager's verbal and written communicating abilities can also be achieved in part by coaching. Also useful can be attendance on formal training courses on public speaking and report writing. In a negotiating context, communication involves the ability to command attention in the course of a discussion, and to handle forceful and possibly hostile pressures from the other side. There is a need, in other words, for a degree of assertiveness which may not come naturally to an inexperienced negotiator. Women, too, may feel inhibited if they are alone or in the minority in an industrial relations arena which has often been dominated by men.

Training courses in assertiveness have become quite widely available in recent years – often in the context of an equal opportunity programme. They have a particular value in negotiation training. The literature on assertiveness has also grown[2,3] and is a useful source of assistance for negotiators who experience difficulty in making an impact on a lively, forceful or fast-moving discussion.

References

[1] LEIGH A. *20 ways to manage better*. London, Institute of Personnel Management. 1984.
[2] BACK K and K. *Assertiveness at work*. Maidenhead, Berks, McGraw-Hill. 1982.
[3] STUBBS D. *How to use assertiveness at work*. Aldershot, Hants, Gower. 1986.

8 Other negotiating modes and strategies

So far, we have concentrated on the negotiating meeting, on negotiation as person to person contact involving verbal communication. Documentation has been referred to mainly to emphasize the importance of confirming the final agreement in writing, though in the last chapter passing mention was made of the possibility of conducting negotiations through correspondence. Brief earlier reference has also been made to the involvement of the media and to the influence of legislation.

The emphasis on meetings, at which the parties discuss and resolve their differences without the intrusion of external influences, reflects the fact that this is by far the most common negotiating mode. There are, however, other modes which are used either as part of the total negotiating process or sometimes as alternatives to meetings. Strategies may also need to take account of, or use the powers of, the media and the law. This chapter therefore examines four issues:

- The use of correspondence: negotiating by letter
- The use of the telephone
- The use and influence of the media
- The use and implications of the law.

The use of correspondence

It is not uncommon for negotiations to be started by correspondence. The trade union writes to the employer requesting a meeting to discuss a claim or complaint. Alternatively, management may initiate a meeting by writing to the union to invite discussion on some pending plan or problem. There are no major difficulties about such preliminary moves, though two points may be borne in mind.

First, not too much need be read into the tone of a union's first letter. It is not unusual for such a letter to be cast in fairly aggressive terms: 'We are seeking an urgent meeting to discuss the very serious situation which has arisen in the despatch department due to management's refusal to supply protective footwear. This is a blatant breach not only of the factory safety agreement but also of the Health and Safety at Work Act. My members are disgusted at the management's attitude to this matter and we will be demanding immediate action to put things right. If this is not forthcoming we will have to consider what action we can take to ensure that proper safety standards are enforced.'

It may well be that the letter has been written by the full-time official in this style only so that it can be shown to the shop steward concerned as evidence that the union is taking the matter seriously. Alternatively, it may have been written by an inexperienced trade unionist who thinks that this is the way to show the management that the union is not going to be pushed around; or perhaps by an official who thinks the management might be panicked into action by this style. (One management negotiator has described this as the Fat Boy syndrome: the character in Dickens' *Pickwick Papers* whose catch-phrase is: 'I makes yer flesh creep!') Come the actual meeting it is quite likely that the tone will be very different – good-humoured, reasonable and flexible. It is easy to be abrupt, abrasive and threatening at a distance, such as in a letter: it is less easy to maintain this stance when talking across the table to managers who retain their courtesy and cool.

The second point is to consider the timing of replies to union letters. It may be that there are good reasons for not rushing into negotiations and delay may therefore be appropriate. It may then seem best simply to sit on the union's letter and make no reply. In most cases this is unwise. It opens the door to a new complaint that the management are being dilatory and discourteous. When the meeting does eventually take place, it will start on a sour note as the union speakers castigate management for the delay. This does not mean that the union can dictate the timing of negotiations. Their initial letter should be replied to fairly promptly, but time can be gained either by suggesting a date for a meeting which is some way off or, more subtly, by hitting the ball back into the union's court with a question or request: 'We are certainly willing to have a meeting, but to avoid any waste of time then, it would be helpful if you could let us have a note of whatever action your shop steward has taken to resolve the matter within the department, together with more detail about the action you think management now needs to initiate. Perhaps you could also explain whether your reference to the despatch department refers just to the loading bay, which according to our records is the only area where the question of safety footwear has previously been discussed.'

This example also illustrates how a complete negotiating episode may be conducted through correspondence. Assume the union official replies giving a fairly detailed account of the background to the complaint and of the remedies sought. The management will then be in a position to investigate and consider the issue, and may conclude that some action is necessary, not exactly what the union is asking for, but at least something. Instead of convening a meeting with the union about this, a further letter might be written: 'Thank you for your recent helpful letter. We have looked into the points you raise and we agree that there is a case for improving the safety precautions on the loading bay. We therefore propose to . . . (giving details of the action proposed). We hope that you can accept that these proposals solve the problem, and if so they can be implemented immediately without the need for any formal meeting.' The union may reply accepting this, or may agree in part while still pressing for some additional action. This, too, might be dealt with in a further exchange of letters: meetings are not the only means of discussion, compromise and agreement.

What are the advantages of negotiating by letter, rather than by meetings? Three main benefits can be suggested:

1   Much time can be saved. Producing a letter, and reading and considering the reply, may well take only, say, 30 minutes. Against this, negotiating meetings are notoriously time-consuming. The safety shoe case, just quoted, might well involve a meeting (or meetings) between three managers and several union officials, and last three hours. The time-saving factor may be just as attractive to an over-pressed full-time union officer as to a busy manager. It is less likely to appeal to a shop steward.

2   A potential emotionally-charged situation might be avoided.

Leaving aside the safety shoe case, in another situation it might be known that while the full-time union officer will be reasonable, the shop steward who would have to attend any meeting has a very highly charged view of the matter under discussion and will use the meeting to mount an aggressive and personalized attack. To avoid this, the full-time officer may, in effect, collude with the management in handling the issue through correspondence.

3 The whole negotiation will be on the record. There may be cases – particularly those with potential legal dimensions – in which it is important that there should be no possibility of misunderstanding or misquoting of who said what when. Conducting the whole bargaining process by correspondence obviously achieves this.

The use of the telephone

This is a more minor point than the use of correspondence, and applies mainly to informal and small scale negotiation involving only two participants. Its main purpose is again as a device to save time.

A trade union official telephones a personnel manager and says: 'Can we fix a date when I can come and put to you what we think ought to be done about how your security people are handling random searches?' It may be wholly appropriate to agree to this request for a meeting and so to plunge straight into a discussion on dates. The experienced manager may, however, be a little more cautious. His or her reply might then be: 'That's an interesting request – what's the problem?' Or perhaps: 'I'm heavily tied up for the next few days; have you got a couple of minutes to have a chat about it on the phone now?'

Either way, there is a possibility, particularly if it is an issue on which such a call is not unexpected, that a 20 minute discussion on the phone might resolve matters. Even if that does not prove possible, the manager may still be able to keep subsequent discussions to the telephone by concluding the first conversation: 'OK – I can't take it further right now, but I'll go into the points you've raised and to save us both time, I'll ring you back as soon as I have an answer.'

There is one other reason for using the telephone in some instances. This is to secure immediate agreement to a proposal or, as was suggested in the last chapter, to clear the draft of a document such as the minutes of a meeting or a written agreement. There is something about the telephone as a medium of communication which has the effect on at least some people of their giving assent far more readily than they ever would in a face to face discussion, or in correspondence. It is not clear why this should be. Perhaps the unexpectedness of a telephone call which interrupts current activity, together with its slightly detached or abstract quality, combined with an underlying feeling that it is not a normal negotiating mode, reduces the usual resistance and caution which are displayed in other modes of communication.

Whatever the reasons, experience indicates that points of detail which can occupy considerable and long-winded discussion at a meeting, may be agreed very quickly in a telephone conversation. So the manager may phone the union official and say: 'Jane, you remember we spoke last month about increasing the motor cycle allowance but left it open as to whether this went up by either 3p or 4p? Well, I've checked out our calculations with the RAC and there really isn't a case for the higher figure as yet. So unless you feel it's a die-in-the-ditch matter, we would like to start paying the extra 3p from tomorrow: can I take it that you wouldn't object?' Put like this, with a tight time scale, an answer invited immediately, and the pressure of other business which the phone call has just interrupted, there is a good chance that the union official's answer will be yes. The danger, of course, is that the answer may instead be a quick no. A negotiator who uses the telephone to get quick results needs to be confident that his or her skill in this mode is greater than that of the other party.

The use of the media

In an earlier chapter two aspects of media involvement were touched on. It was pointed out that there are many objections to negotiating through the media, but that there has been a trend in recent years for employers and trade unions to make more use of the media to explain and argue their respective positions.

The media's own interest is rarely in negotiations as such. The main interest is in the drama of conflict: strikes, picketing, the clash of old and new technology. Only the specialist writers in the quality press attempt any real analysis of what are frequently the highly complex issues under negotiation, though superficial attempts may be made to clarify these issues. On both national and local TV or radio, there have been many occasions in which the main protagonists in a pay dispute have been brought together with an interviewer who, in a two minute spot, asks the employer: 'So far you have offered only x per cent, the union have said they want at least y per cent, so how much more are you willing to offer?' The standard employer response is: 'This is not the time or place to answer that question.' The interviewer then turns to the trade union official and asks: 'So far your strike action does not seem to have had much effect: what are you going to do next to persuade the employers to move?' To which the standard trade union answer is: 'My executive committee will be considering this shortly.' A barren exchange of this kind does not seem of particular benefit to either party, nor would it appear to be of riveting interest to the general public.

In that example, however, the initiative for the TV or radio interview lay with the broadcasting organization. A producer will have telephoned the two protagonists and asked them to appear. Each may have done so reluctantly, possibly only after having been told (not necessarily in truth) that the other person has already agreed. Neither may have given any real thought as to how their appearance might be used positively. Both may have acted defensively, against each other and against the interviewer.

The media can be used much more positively than this, though not as a mode of negotiation as such. A TV or radio studio is no place for all the cut and thrust and subtleties of the bargaining process. But that process can be influenced in two ways in which skilled use of the media can assist.

First, press, radio and TV can be used to disseminate factual information, the wide knowledge of which will help to promote understanding and therefore support for the employer's position.

Secondly, this support can be enhanced by the use of the media to project an appropriate style or image.

In planning to use the media for these purposes, it must be remembered that there are two audiences which overlap, the general public and the employees. Public opinion, public attitudes, can have an important influence on employees in at least some types of dispute. Public utility workers, for example, may have an exceedingly uncomfortable time with neighbours during a water or electricity strike. Even in a much less direct case, a general feeling that the public are sympathetic − or antagonistic − will have a conditioning effect on employees' attitudes towards the degree of vigour with which they will pursue a claim, and towards their acceptance of a compromise settlement.

But because employees are part of the public, the employer must be careful not to portray a position through the media which is blatantly biased or inaccurate. That will not only generate adverse employee reaction, it will probably become public knowledge that gross distortion is occurring − hardly the public image which will best serve the aim of obtaining public support.

Generally speaking, then, the characteristics of an employer's media messages should be:

Accuracy: facts and figures should be correct and capable, if challenged, of ready proof

Clarity: however complex the situation, the key points must be picked out and explained in simple, direct language

Reasonableness: the tone is best kept unemotive and 'commonsensical'. This does not imply a flat or uninteresting style; what is needed is a down-to-earth, lively, positive approach − goodwill and sweet reason, not rancour or rhetoric.

There are a number of methods of getting one's case into the media, including making better use of the invited interview:

Press advertisements. There is only one way to retain total control of the wording and presentation of a message and avoid any editorial cutting or paraphrasing − to buy advertising space. National examples in recent years have included the Coal Board and British Rail. If the advantage is total control, the disadvantage is that the advertisement format carries less conviction than editorial comment or a news item. People take all advertisements with a pinch of salt. In drafting this form of pronouncement, it is important to decide whether it is to be aimed primarily at the general public, or specifically at employees.

Press releases. A press release is a prepared statement which is issued to newspapers, TV and radio stations for them to use as they see fit. Some may use it unedited and without editorial comment, merely saying: 'Messrs XYZ plc announced today that . . . (quoting the release in full) . . .' Frequently, however, the release will be used selectively, with extracts from it inbedded in a media-written news story. There is no guarantee, either, that it will be used at all. That depends on the media's view of the item's newsworthiness.

Press releases which stand the best chance of being used with minimum editorial interference are those which tell a story simply and clearly, and which, if at all possible, are personalized. To illustrate this, here is the opening part of a release which the media largely ignored:

'Messrs YXZ plc regret to announce that despite their offer of significant improvements to the proposals they put to the trade union last week, it proved impossible at a lengthy meeting this morning to persuade the unions to call off their current industrial action. This was despite an offer partially to consolidate attendance allowances within the bonus calculator which would have had a multiplying effect on average earnings . . .'

This statement is dull, impersonal and, except to the industrial relations specialist, all but meaningless. It would have stood a better chance of being used if it had been written thus:

'Speaking at the end of a long meeting with trade union secretary John Brown this morning, Adrian Green, XYZ's 35 year old managing director, said: "We're almost at the end of the line in this dispute. We upped our offer from around five per cent to a package which would boost the average pay packet by nearly seven per cent but the union wouldn't budge an inch from their original 10 per cent claim. They say the strike goes on, but we think it's time they gave their members a chance to have second thoughts" . . .'

Press conferences. If it is thought that the matter is of considerable interest to the media, the issue of a press release or official statement can be combined with a press conference. Press, radio and TV reporters are invited to attend at a fixed date and time, and are told that a statement will be made, followed by a question and answer session. It is best to select a venue convenient to the media – a town centre hotel, for example, rather than the company conference room if this is out of town. It is also normal to lay on light refreshments – and to say so when issuing the invitations to attend.

The advantage of the press conference is that it provides an opportunity to provide far more explanation and comment than can be included in a short, pithy press statement. The two possible disadvantages are first, that no one may turn up; second, that the questioning is unpredictable and may be hostile, or touch on issues which the employer wants to keep under wraps.

The radio or TV interview. Interviews are usually initiated by the broadcasting station but may also be suggested by the interviewee. Local radio and TV particularly are often desperate to fill up air time. There is no reason why an employer with something to say should not telephone the local station and suggest an interview. The idea might be rejected, but there is no harm in trying. Either way, it is risky to embark on radio or TV interviews without some basic training or professional advice. There are numerous short courses on offer by colleges or other training organizations which provide such tuition. Some local TV stations are also willing to run short training sessions for local employers (and trade unions).

By whatever means such interviews are initiated, it is of vital importance that the interviewees are very clear, in advance, of just one, or at the most two, key points to be got across in the interview regardless of what questions may be asked. A media interview is an opportunity to give a message, be this a fact, opinion or suggestion. It is not a test of one's ability to give away as little as possible under interrogation. This does not mean, however, that all that can be done is to give direct answers to the interviewer's questions. He or she is unlikely, in fact, to ask precisely the right question to get the key point across. One needs, therefore, to prepare a short, crisp statement which includes a lead out of whatever question might be asked.

As an example, take the case quoted above as a press release. The managing director is asked to be interviewed on his local television station's regional news programme. He decides that the one point he needs to get across is that it is the trade union's turn to make a concession. Management has negotiated in good faith and have moved twice towards the union's position. The union have stuck on their original claim – and that's not playing the game.

So, mentally, he prepares an all-purpose answer. In the event, the interviewer's first question is: 'Mr Green, you were not able to settle the strike at your meeting this morning, so what are you going to do next?' Green's reply is: 'The real issue is when is the union going to show some flexibility. We have moved twice towards them, now it's for them to come towards us.' This is an answer which with very little amendment can be used for any question the interviewer is likely to put. If the union official is being interviewed at the same time it will probably result in the interviewer turning this rather awkward point onto the union. If the manager is being interviewed on his own, the interviewer will probably follow the point up and so provide the manager with an opportunity of reinforcing it.

The use and influence of the law

The law does not have a direct impact on the detailed conduct of negotiations. There is no legislation or case law which specifies how negotiations should or should not be progressed. There are, however, two broad areas of the law which need to be kept in mind, either as background information to avoid possible pitfalls, or at times as potential aids to the strengthening of the employer's bargaining or power position. In summary these areas are:

- The relationship between agreements and contract law
- The law regarding trade union immunity from claims for damages caused by industrial action, or from injunctions.

The first point – the implications of contract law – is important in relation to the conclusion, drafting, implementation and enforcement of the outcome of negotiations, that is to say, collective agreements.

The second point, trade union immunities, has a bearing on the assessment of the relative strength of the employer's and trade union's positions should sanctions be threatened or introduced to support the negotiating process.

Contract law

Collective agreements themselves are presumed at law not to be legally binding unless they include a specific term to the contrary. In this respect, agreements between employers and trade unions are treated by the law quite differently from all other forms of agreement. In the commercial world, for example, a negotiated price agreement will be presumed to be binding as a legal contract even if it is only verbal. Provided there is reasonable proof of its existence, its terms are enforceable in the civic courts. Not so even with the most formally drafted of collective agreements. There is no bar on an employer and trade union making an agreement legally binding. All that is needed is the inclusion in writing of a clause to this effect. The almost total absence of such agreements is a result, not of the law, but of the strength of custom and practice, and of the traditional dislike, particularly by the trade unions, of the involvement of the courts in industrial relations. Between December 1971 and July 1974 the law made an opposite assumption – that collective agreements were legally binding unless they included a clause saying they were not. This attempt by government to introduce more legal discipline into the enforcement of agreements failed totally. It became standard practice to include what was known as a 'TINA LEA' clause in all agreements – 'This Is Not a Legally Enforceable Agreement.' There are signs in 1986 that some employers and one or two unions are cautiously interested in moving away from the traditional position, but the general picture is still that neither party to a collective agreement can sue the other for breach (or enforcement) of contract.

This does not mean, however, that the employer is free from all such actions. Most collective agreements are incorporated by one means or another into employees' contracts of employment. Individual employees are then able to compel their employer to enforce the application of the relevant terms of their contracts.

Collective agreements can be imported into individual contracts of employment either expressly or impliedly:

Express incorporation requires a direct statement to that effect in the contract of employment, for example: 'Your terms and conditions of employment will be those set out in the agreements concluded between the company and the TGWU as amended from time to time.' It should be noted that where national and local agreements are in use, reference should be made to both in this type of contractual clause.

In the absence of an express clause of this type, there are still circumstances in which the courts may decide that an employee's contract includes terms from a *collective agreement by implication*. The employee would have to show that it was well-established by custom and practice to apply the terms of agreements in this way. To quote legal jargon, this practice would have to be 'notorious, certain and reasonable.' This means that the application of the terms of agreements would have to be common knowledge to the employees concerned, that there would have to be certainty as to which employees the agreement applied to and which precise terms were involved, and that these terms were not so unreasonable that it was improbable that employees would have accepted them.

This question of the implied incorporation of the terms of an agreement in individual contracts can be a matter of some importance in an only partially unionized workforce, perhaps with several unions covering a rather complicated mixture of occupations. Is it absolutely clear in such cases as to whom each agreement applies? Do non-unionist employees understand and accept that their conditions of service derive from collective agreements and, if so, which?

To avoid misunderstandings, and possible legal difficulties, it seems best to be specific about this matter, and to state clearly in contracts of employment which agreements are used to define individual conditions of employment.

In both the express and implied cases, one other point needs to be understood: the situation which arises when agreements are altered, or when the employer unilaterally withdraws from them. Changes to agreements which are themselves agreed do not cause contractual problems provided it is clear (expressly or impliedly) that such changes are automatically incorporated into individual contracts. Hence the phrase 'as may be amended from time to time' in the example of an express clause, quoted above. But if the employer withdraws from an agreement or a clause in an agreement unilaterally, the situation may be very different. The trade union cannot sue for breach of the agreement, but individual employees may sue for breach of contract. In 1983, British Gas withdrew a previously negotiated bonus scheme. Gas fitters successfully sued, on the basis that this unilateral termination of an agreement which was expressly incorporated in their contracts of employment did not change their individual contractual rights.

Trade union immunities

An important element in the balance of negotiating power, discussed in the opening chapters of this book, is the ability of trade unions to damage the employer by industrial action. The threat or possibility of this sanction lies behind many union claims and has a direct or indirect influence on employers' negotiating strategies. It is therefore of importance in considering strategy to assess the extent, if at all, to which this aspect of union power and pressure might be reduced. One possible means of achieving such reduction is by taking legal action, a means which employment legislation in the 80s has widened.

Two main legal remedies are open to employers to combat trade union power in some circumstances:

1   *Injunctions.* These are orders of the court to desist from, or to take, certain specified action. For example, to cease the blacking of supplies, or to issue instructions to a union district office to publish ballot results. Injunctions are very powerful instruments as to disobey them amounts to contempt of court, and the court has unlimited power to impose penalties for this offence, eg imprisonment, punitive fines.

2   *Damages.* Unless they have immunity, trade unions can be sued for financial losses incurred by an employer as a result of industrial action. There are statutory limits on the amount of such damages, depending on the size of the union. The range is from £10,000 for a union with less than 5,000 members, to £250,000 for a union with 250,000 or more members.

These remedies cannot be sought in all circumstances. Their use is limited to cases in which the union's normal legal immunity from such civil action is withdrawn by the provisions of the relevant legislation. This applies in two main instances:

1   Where the union has failed to conduct a ballot of all the employees concerned within the four weeks prior to endorsing or authorizing the industrial action. The legislation specifies in some detail how the ballot must be conducted.

2   Where the industrial action is 'secondary'. This applies to action

against an employer who is not connected with the particular dispute.

The legislation relating to trade union immunities is very complex. Its definitions and the interpretations of the courts regarding secondary industrial action are particularly complicated and are still evolving. This book is not the place for the very lengthy legal exposition which would be needed to cover the subject comprehensively. The purpose of referring to the subject in a book on negotiation is to provide a reminder that this is an aspect which in some disputes may merit detailed review when planning a negotiating strategy. Expert legal advice is essential if an employer is seriously considering going to the courts for the remedies and in the circumstances sketched briefly in this chapter.

On a less formal or definitive basis, management negotiators may nevertheless find it helpful at least to let the union negotiators see that they are aware of these relatively new legal provisions. The union leader might begin to drop hints of immediate industrial action. The management might respond: 'You do know that we could do the union for damages unless you hold a secret ballot?' Whether such a comment would improve or exacerbate the negotiating situation is, as is true of all the examples and quotes in this book, a matter for judgement at the particular time.

The right to information

One other statutory provision must be mentioned, although it does not loom large in most negotiations.[1] It is the right given to trade unions to be supplied by the employer with such information 'without which a trade union representative would be impeded to a material extent in bargaining.' There are safeguards for the employer against the disclosure of confidential and trade information. The type of information involved is that 'which it would be in accordance with good industrial relations practice to disclose.' The information must have some relevance to the issues under negotiation, and is limited to matters on which the union concerned has bargaining rights. In general, this provision covers information about pay scales, average earnings, relevant productivity data and the like – information which most employers either disclose already or have no objection to disclosing if asked.

Difficulties occur when it is unclear as to what matters the employer has accepted as negotiable with the trade union concerned, or where there is a lack of clarity as to which employees the trade union has been recognized as representing for collective bargaining purposes. Occasionally, too, a trade union looking to extend its sphere of influence may embark on a 'fishing expedition', asking for a whole range of information in the hope that somewhere within this data it may find some useful ammunition for its campaign.

The statutory provisions (Employment Protection Act, 1975) are supplemented by a code of practice issued by the Advisory Conciliation and Arbitration Service (ACAS). ACAS also play a part in any formally notified dispute in which a trade union claims that an employer is refusing to supply relevant information. A claim of this kind has to be made to the Central Arbitration Committee (CAC). The CAC then has to refer the case to ACAS who must attempt to resolve the dispute by conciliation (see next chapter for an explanation of ACAS' conciliation role). Only if ACAS cannot help the union and employer to resolve the dispute does the case go to a formal CAC hearing. The CAC then rules on which information (if any) the employer should disclose. Somewhat surprisingly, this CAC ruling is not directly enforceable at law. There is no way in which an employer can be forced by law to disclose any information whatsoever.

If the employer does refuse to disclose even the information to which the CAC has ruled that the union has a right, the union's legal remedy is to submit a claim for some improvement in the pay or conditions of service of the employees concerned. This claim goes to the CAC – it does not have to be the subject of prior negotiations with the employer. The CAC then assesses whether the claim is reasonable, taking into account evidence from both parties and, if so, makes an award specifying what the new pay or other conditions of service should be. This award is enforceable against the employer, though again by a somewhat indirect means. The terms specified by the CAC are deemed to be incorporated into the employees' contracts of employment. If the employer refuses to apply them, the CAC takes no action. It is for the employees as individuals to take their employer to the county court for breach of contract.

In practice, this peculiarly long-winded process is very rarely followed. Almost all formally notified disputes about the disclosure of information are settled either by conciliation, or by employers accepting the CAC's rulings.

If faced with a union demand for information, backed by reference to their statutory rights, there are six tests to be applied to determine whether the information concerned falls within the statutory provisions:

1   Is it needed for current bargaining? The information must be relevant to a real, current bargaining need, not just of general interest or possible future use.

2   Would negotiations be seriously hampered without it? The union must show that the lack of this information would significantly impede its ability to negotiate.

3   Is it in the employer's possession? The union cannot demand information which the employer does not have, however useful such data might be.

4   Is it about the employer's undertaking? There are no rights to information about other employers or about matters extraneous to the employer's own business.

5   Is it good industrial relations practice to give such information? If the requested information is of a kind which most good employers would disclose as a matter of course, refusal may be difficult to sustain. Conversely, if the union is asking for something unusual in an industrial relations context, their claim will probably be weak.

The statutory definition of collective bargaining

6   The sixth point is a general one – that the whole of the statutory provision about disclosure applies only in the context of collective bargaining – which is itself subject to statutory definition.

The Employment Protection Act, 1975, defines collective bargaining as 'negotiations relating to or connected with one or more of the matters specified in section 29(1) of the Trade Union and Labour Relations Act, 1974.'

The reference to the 1974 Act is to its statutory definition of a 'trade dispute'. Only when industrial action results from a trade dispute as so defined does a trade union acquire the immunities discussed earlier in this chapter. The definition states that a trade dispute is a dispute between workers and their employer which is wholly or mainly about one of the following matters – and these matters therefore also constitute the subject matter of collective bargaining in accordance with the 1975 Act and the unions' rights to information:

- Terms and conditions of employment
- Physical working conditions
- The engagement, non-engagement, termination or suspension of employment of one or more workers
- Matters of discipline
- Membership or non-membership of trade unions
- Facilities for trade union officials
- The machinery for negotiation or consultation
- Trade union recognition.

This is a fairly comprehensive schedule and most normal negotiations fall within its definitions. It does, however, leave some ambiguities or uncertainties. Would negotiations about the content of a training course, for example, fall within any of the scheduled topics? No generally definitive answer can be given: each case has to be judged on its merits. It is certainly possible, though, to envisage a trade union requesting information under the Act which the employer could legitimately hold to be outside this statutory definition of the subject matter of collective bargaining.

Reference

[1] For a comprehensive explanation of statute and case law, see: *Disclosing bargaining information.* IDS Brief, Incomes Data Services, February 1979.

9 Handling breakdown

The negotiating process is not always successful. It may prove impossible to reach agreement, and the problem then arises as to what alternative courses of action should be considered. Essentially, this comes down to a choice between seeking external third party assistance, or attempting to procede unilaterally.

This is an important choice because it must be recognized that the outcome of any form of third party involvement will probably be some further movement beyond the position reached when the negotiations broke down. If the management position reached at that time really does represent the absolute limit of what can be offered or accepted, then third party assistance is dangerous. It will probably lead to pressure for further compromise, and if the management resists this and sticks firmly to its closing position at the time of breakdown, it is likely to be seen as obstructive and intransigent. The psychological pressure to accept compromise is very strong.

One option, therefore, is to ignore the breakdown and carry on. How practicable this is depends partly on the nature of the disputed issue, partly on where the initiative and power lies for further action. If the subject of negotiation is a straightforward pay claim, the employer has no action to take to sustain a failure to reach agreement. Wages will continue to be paid at the old rates and it will be for the trade union to decide whether or not it is able to effect any form of additional pressure (by strike action, for example) to force the employer back to the negotiating table. If the dispute is about a management initiative (such as the introduction of new technology) the employer will have to assess whether or not the objective can be achieved without the agreement and co-operation of the trade union. The only general principle involved is the balance of power, and that is a matter which can be assessed only on a case by case basis.

It may be realized, however, that it is improbable that the position extant at the time of breakdown is sustainable. It may be evident that the union is in a position to inflict significant damage by industrial action, or that there are significant practical difficulties in attempting to take unilateral action to enforce a management plan. At the same time, all conceivable proposals and counter-proposals have been made and rejected. It is in these circumstances that third party assistance should be considered.

Such assistance can be obtained in three forms:

1   *Conciliation:* in which the conciliator assists the parties to reach their own eventual agreement.

2   *Mediation:* in which the mediator suggests a solution which the parties may accept or reject.

3   *Arbitration:* in which the parties agree in advance to accept the arbitrator's solution.

In practice, conciliation may shade into mediation, though it is advisable for the parties to understand in advance the extent to which the conciliator may take the initiative in offering solutions for consideration.

Participation in both conciliation and mediation is entirely voluntary. There is no obligation, other than a moral one, to accept the outcome. But arbitration, while voluntarily entered into, does require a commitment to accept and implement the arbitrator's decision (or, as it is normally termed, the arbitration award).

In choosing which of these three forms of third party help should be sought, the effects of the three different processes need to be considered. Conciliation comes closest to normal negotiation, and provides the most scope for retaining initiative and control over the outcome. Mediation is similar, but may result in significant pressure to accept the mediator's solution which may be less acceptable than anything the management might eventually have evolved. In arbitration, the parties have no control over the eventual outcome. They may influence it by the force of the cases they put to the arbitrator, but at the end of the day they have no say in the actual award. In consequence, arbitration is the most risky of the three forms, each of which is examined in more detail later in this chapter.

Before doing so it is necessary to explain the role of the Advisory

Conciliation and Arbitration Service (ACAS) as it is through this body that most employers and trade unions obtain third party assistance. Not that there is any statutory requirement to seek ACAS' aid, or that such services are available only from ACAS. It is open to any employer and trade union to agree to obtain conciliation or arbitration assistance from any quarter. Some organizations and industries have standing domestic arrangements to this end, often calling on the services of jointly respected academics or lawyers for this purpose. ACAS, however, are used in the overwhelming majority of cases, and their methods of operation form a model for all third party functions.

The Advisory Conciliation and Arbitration Service (ACAS)

ACAS is a body established by statute (Employment Protection Act, 1975) and funded by government. Its Chairman is appointed by the Secretary of State for Employment. The government plays no part, however, in its actual operations and has no powers of involvement in, or direction of, its affairs. To operate successfully, as ACAS does, it has to be seen by employers and trade unions as independent of government, and impartial.

ACAS' governing board includes employer and trade union members, but the Service's day-to-day work is undertaken by its full time staff, operating from a London Headquarters and a network of regional offices.

ACAS' conciliation role is defined by statute. The Service has a duty to offer collective conciliation either when asked by one or more of the parties to a dispute, or on its own initiative. It is important to note that either party to a dispute – usually after negotiations have broken down – can ask for ACAS' assistance; the request does not have to be a joint one. Of course, if only one party to a dispute makes such a request, ACAS will approach the other party to seek their co-operation. Similarly, if ACAS observe a dispute occurring and offer conciliation assistance before either party asks for it, the Service will approach both sides to see if each will agree to ACAS involvement.

The precise nature of ACAS conciliation varies from case to case. In small scale disputes it may consist of the part-time involvement of just one member of the relevant regional staff. In major national disputes, handled through ACAS' London Headquarters, a team of ACAS officials may be involved. Conciliation by its very nature is an informal process and there are no formal procedures which have to be followed.

One other form of conciliation is defined by statute. It is a legal requirement that every complaint of unfair dismissal (and most other cases concerning applications to the industrial tribunals about individual employment rights) is referred to ACAS regional offices. ACAS have a duty to attempt conciliated settlements before such cases are heard by the tribunals. ACAS deal with upwards of 30,000 such cases annually, and achieve settlements in about 40 per cent of them.

Neither in these individual cases, nor in collective disputes, is there any statutory obligation on the parties themselves to accept ACAS conciliation. ACAS has a duty to offer help; there is no legal requirement to agree to this.

Formally, mediation is a different process and involves the appointment of a mediator who discusses the issue with both parties and eventually produces a recommended solution. In some ACAS conciliations, ACAS officials may, on an informal basis, go quite a long way towards offering their own solutions. To what extent that occurs during conciliation is a matter for agreement and acceptance by all concerned. More formally, both parties may prefer in advance to seek mediation rather than conciliation or arbitration. They may want a fresh view on the disputed issue from someone whose opinions and recommendations they can both respect. If ACAS is asked to assist with mediation this is not normally provided by ACAS' own staff. Instead, ACAS appoints an independent person (or sometimes a small board), drawn from lists of suitable persons.

A similar procedure is followed by ACAS if the parties seek arbitration. ACAS maintains lists of persons suitable to serve as either single arbitrators or on arbitration boards. It is normal for the choice of arbitrators to be discussed by ACAS with the parties to a dispute, and it is open to each party to suggest names, which may not necessarily be on the ACAS lists. A very standard format for an arbitration board is for the chairperson to be an academic or a lawyer, supported by one employer representative and one trade union representative – both the latter being drawn from organizations wholly independent of either of the parties to the dispute.

Conciliation

Conciliation, whether provided by ACAS or some other source, has little chance of being effective unless both parties are prepared to consider the possibility of some movement, however small, in their own positions. It is not the job of the conciliator to convince one party of the correctness of the other's position. The essence of conciliation is to break the deadlock which has occurred and get the parties back together again, evolving their own agreed solution.

Negotiations break down for a number of reasons other than the impersonal facts of the disputed issue. Emotional outbreaks and personalized attacks on each side's integrity may have occurred, souring the atmosphere and generating such strong feelings of pride and resentment that constructive discussion has become impossible. A lack of imagination or ingenuity on one or both sides may have shut off possible avenues of compromise. One side or the other may have stated their 'final' position too quickly and too publicly so that too much loss of face is involved in being seen to make further movement.

The conciliator's task is to unblock such obstacles to progress. How is this done? In most cases, the conciliator will start by meeting each side separately, seeking each party's explanation both of the issue at stake, and of the perceived reasons for the breakdown in negotiations. At this stage, the conciliator is trying to get each party to distinguish between the critical and peripheral factors: what are each side's key objectives and real sticking points? The conciliator will then probably shuttle between the parties, playing back to each the main points raised by the other, though being careful to respect any confidences which may be involved. At the same time, he or she will be asking questions which might help to show how constructive negotiations might be resumed. For example, the management side, in a case dealing with a package union claim for improved pay and conditions, might be told by the conciliator: 'I've had a long talk with the union side and I get the impression that they resented very strongly your complete rejection of any move on annual leave. They think you have failed so far to deal with the detailed case they put to you about this, and that you may not have realized that they give the leave question a higher priority than one or two of the other items on which you have made offers. Had you seen the situation this way? If not, is it something you might feel able to reconsider?'

What may eventually emerge from the conciliator's exploration with each side separately of their own and of the other's position is the tentative definition of an area for further negotiation. In the example just quoted it might be a possible repackaging of proposals regarding annual leave, shift allowances and sick pay, though without any change to what was on the table in respect of working hours and pay. Given that each side is willing at least to resume talking about the defined issues, it is for them to decide whether they will do so without the involvement of the conciliator. In many cases, both parties find it helpful for at least the first resumed meeting after breakdown to be chaired by the conciliator. The conciliator's role in the chair is to keep the meeting on an even keel, to encourage constructive debate – not to act in any quasi-executive capacity by tabling new proposals. The whole emphasis in conciliation is for the parties to evolve their own solution.

The extent to which a conciliator shuttles between the two separated sides, rather than acting as a facilitating chairperson in a joint meeting, is a matter for his or her judgement. Sometimes, particularly when personal relationships between the management and trade union sides are very bad, they may be kept separate almost until the final agreement. In such instances, the conciliator will go as far as relaying suggested concessions from one party to the other, and seeking a response: 'The unions would be willing to consider agreeing to only one extra day's leave, provided you made an acceptable improvement in sick pay. Is this something you are prepared to consider? If so, have you a provisional proposition I might relay to the union as a basis for agreement?'

It can be seen from this description of the conciliation process that the conciliator needs to demonstrate complete impartiality in order to retain the confidence of both sides, and to display very considerable qualities of integrity and tact. There may be a temptation at times for the conciliator to 'cheat' by exploiting the separate meetings with each side. It would be possible, for example, to tell each side of some alleged provisional concession from the other, just to explore the reaction and possibly find a new way forward. But if either side eventually discovers that the conciliator has resorted to such deception, and has failed honestly to relay their views and proposals to the other party, the credibility of that conciliator would be wholly destroyed. It is greatly to the credit of ACAS that it has established an unsullied reputation for maintaining these high qualities of integrity and impartiality with employers and trade unions.

Mediation

The principle of mediation has already been explained in the section above describing ACAS' services. It is best seen as being mid-way between conciliation and arbitration, both in formality and in the degree of initiative and influence vested in the third party.

Although mediators are free to come up with proposals which are wholly different from those either of the parties may have previously considered, effective mediators will want to lay the foundation for acceptance rather than rejection of their proposals. They are therefore likely to spend more time in discussion with the parties than arbitrators do, while at the same time avoiding being drawn into negotiation. This can be a delicate line to sustain. If the mediator says to the trade union: 'What is your reaction likely to be to any proposal to alter the present shift schedules?' a wily trade union will try to get more details before committing itself, or will immediately tie a condition to any tentative interest: 'We might be willing to look at it, provided there was some improvement in actual earnings.' In such a discussion, the mediator is being treated by the union as a party to negotiate with, which is not the purpose of mediation. In consequence, mediators may lean closer to arbitration procedures in which the third party role is more detached than in conciliation.

Arbitration

The essence of arbitration is that both parties place their fortunes entirely in the hands of the arbitrators by committing themselves in advance to accepting the arbitration award. Because collective agreements are not legally binding, an agreement to go to arbitration does not imply that the arbitration award can be enforced against an unwilling party in the courts. The acceptance of arbitration awards is a matter of honour and integrity, not of statutory or contractual obligation. The principle is so clearly understood, however, that it is extremely rare for an arbitration award to be rejected by either an employer or trade union. After all, if the two sides want to see a third party solution, but do not want to commit themselves in advance to accepting it, they can seek mediation, rather than arbitration.

The arbitration process itself is always more formal than conciliation. It is standard practice in cases set up by ACAS for the procedure to follow this pattern:

The parties are expected to agree the terms of reference for the arbitration.

Each party is asked to submit a full written case statement to the arbitrators.

Once both statements have been received, the arbitrators send each party the other's statement. So neither has any advantage in seeing the other's case before writing their own statement, but both know what is in each other's statement before the arbitration hearing.

The arbitration hearing, while relatively informal in tone, follows a set procedure. Each party in turn is asked to make a verbal presentation of their own case. Each is given the opportunity of commenting on the other's written case, and this may involve the tabling of additional documentation to rebut statements in the opposing case. As in a court or tribunal, any such additional 'evidence' must be copied to the other party who will be able to comment on it.

The arbitrator (or members of the arbitration board) then questions each side in turn about their written and verbal statements.

After this question session, each party is given the opportunity of making a closing statement, commenting on anything which may have arisen during questions, and generally summing up.

The arbitrator or the board then considers the case and in due course produces a written award which is sent to both parties. It is not unusual for there to be a period of several weeks between the arbitration hearing and the announcement of the award.

Arbitrators vary in the extent to which, in their written awards, they explain the reasons for their decisions. These are sometimes given quite fully, but may equally be wholly omitted. There is a school of thought which says that the more an award is explained, the greater the possibility that a disappointed party will find some flaw in the arbitrator's reasoning, and therefore have an excuse to reject the award.

It is evident from this description of the process, that the preparation of a clearly written, well argued case statement is of the utmost importance. It is on this that the arbitrators will concentrate, treating the verbal contributions very much as supplementary to, and supportive of, the written case. In preparing this statement it must also be remembered that the trade union side will be sent it, and will have the time to identify any flaws of fact or logic.

The other side of this coin is that the management will also have the union's written statement, and should subject this to the closest possible scrutiny so that its weaknesses can be drawn to the arbitrator's attention. Many of the skills involved in preparing written statements, analysing them for flaws, and presenting them to an arbitration board, are similar to those exercised by barristers in the courts. For this reason, employers sometimes retain Counsel to lead for them in arbitration hearings. There is one danger, however, in using legal representation. The arbitrators, in their usually penetrating question session, may well probe factors which do not figure in the formal statements. They may want to know, for example, about a company's general employment philosophy, or about background events. Even the most eminent of QCs will be unable to answer such questions satisfactorily. It is usual, therefore, to send a team to an arbitration hearing, so that direct evidence can be given about any aspect which the arbitrators may raise. Counsel may present the case, and highlight flaws in the other side's statement, but one or more managers will also be there to assist in dealing with other points and to ensure that the arbitration board can get immediate and practical answers. While there may be some similarities in procedure to those of a court or tribunal, the arbitrators are concerned with the realities of industrial relations, not with legalistic niceties or point-scoring.

Arbitration is sometimes criticized for being a long-winded method of arriving at a simple solution – often alleged to be 'splitting the difference'. The trade union sticks on a 10 per cent pay claim. The employers will not budge from five per cent. After all the formalities and delay of arbitration, the award is for seven and a half per cent. It is probable but not inevitable that, in most cases, the arbitration award is likely to lie between the two parties' closing positions. In any event, a study of awards does not support the criticism that the predictable outcome is the half-way position. Occasionally, an award will be wholly for or against one side's case. In the large number of cases where the award is between the two, there have been many instances of decisions being much closer to one side than the other. Indeed, the strongest reason for being wary of using arbitration is the unpredictability of the outcome.

There has been some discussion in recent years about the use of pendulum arbitration, that is where the arbitrator is bound to favour one party, rather than producing any form of compromise solution. Despite its superficial attraction, pendulum arbitration has not been adopted as yet on any significant scale, and it has been criticized as being too simplistic by Sir John Wood, Chairman of the Central Arbitration Committee.

10 Managerial and commercial negotiation

Many of the principles and practices involved in collective bargaining apply equally to negotiations outside the industrial relations arena. Setting objectives, determining an appropriate strategy, weighing up strengths and weaknesses, and most of the tactics of bargaining, all apply with varying degrees of formality or system, whether the negotiations are with a trade union about a wage claim, or between managers who are arguing over a new office layout, or between seller and buyer in the commercial market place, or between two parties' solicitors who are trying to resolve a claim for damages.

The parallel can, however, be taken too far. Each negotiating arena has some characteristics of its own which alter the style or emphases of successful negotiation. To take just one example, the sanctions which form part of the underlying power structure are very different between the industrial relations and managerial or commercial worlds. Part of a trade union's power derives from its ability, through industrial action, to stop the employer's operations. Knowledge of that power, or assessments of its possible use, influence the attitudes of both parties to collective bargaining even if no direct threats are made about its use. Two managers attempting to resolve a difference of view about, say, pricing policy for a new product, do not have such dramatic or obvious sanctions available. Their relative power positions will probably be much more subtle. In commercial bargaining, the equivalent of industrial action is for one party to break off negotiations and leave the scene. That is not an option for the employer or trade union and, as a result, collective bargaining is sometimes more protracted, more complex and more likely to involve large-scale compromise than in the simpler forms of price negotiation in which buyer, seller, or both may readily be able to find alternative customers or suppliers.

This chapter examines the particular characteristics of two forms of negotiation in which many managers become involved:

Managerial negotiation: As was pointed out in the opening chapter, informal negotiation, in the sense of one manager influencing and persuading another, is part of everyday managerial life. This area of negotiation is predominantly informal, although more formal bargaining may occur when management teams meet to thrash out policy changes, or to resolve significant resource allocations.

Commercial negotiation: Bargaining between organizations about prices, product or service delivery, collaborative working and the like, forms the core of commercial activity. Much of this area of negotiation is influenced, directly or indirectly, by the principle of 'the contract' – of offer and acceptance, and of the obligations which this implies.

Managerial negotiation

Managers may negotiate with each other without consciously classifying such interaction as negotiation. A manager in one function or department needs information, or action, or support from a manager elsewhere in the organization. A discussion ensues in which the first manager attempts to persuade the second to co-operate. This type of transaction is brought within the purview of this book because it meets the essence of negotiation as suggested in the definition discussed in the first chapter. Skill in handling this particular form of managerial activity is of critical importance. It is difficult to envisage a highly successful manager who has not mastered the arts of managerial persuasion, and these arts are very much those of the skilled negotiator. There are four major influences on the character and outcomes of this form of negotiation:

● The relative status of the managers involved
● The use of 'connections' with sources of power
● The creation of obligations
● The power of knowledge or expertise.

Status: The influence of differences in formal status on the outcome of discussions between a senior and subordinate manager is very direct. However powerfully the junior of the two may argue, the senior has the authority ultimately to overrule the other's position and to impose a decision. Negotiation in the sense in which it is defined in this book cannot really take place between managers at different levels in the organizational hierarchy who are in an executive or line relationship to each other. Many of the skills of negotiation may be used to good effect by junior managers when trying to persuade their bosses to agree to a particular point of view, but the ultimate right of the boss to make the final decision is an underlying influence which distinguishes this type of managerial transaction from real negotiation.

The situation is different when managers from different parts of an organization meet for discussions. Here, neither manager will have executive authority over the other and, in theory, the resolution of issues on which each initially holds different views should be determined by the logic of the situation, uninfluenced by any status considerations. In reality, the managers' relative status often has an effect.

Take, for example, a young personnel officer whose organizational position is in the third tier in the management hierarchy and who is in a middle managerial salary grade. She is trying to persuade the 60 year old purchasing manager to attend an equal opportunities seminar. He is in the second managerial tier, and is on a higher salary grade. He is reluctant to agree, though he knows that it is company policy that he should, sooner or later, attend a seminar of this kind, so the personnel officer is by no means powerless. He may nevertheless adopt the same tone of seniority in his attitude towards the personnel officer as he would if a very junior member of his own staff came up with an unacceptable idea. His whole attitude, though not his actual words, projects the message that: 'I am more important than you – I'm older, more senior, paid more, and I'm a man. Go away, young lady, and don't bother me with trivia!' This is, of course, an extreme example. Status influence is being exerted on the basis not just of formal organizational seniority, but also on assumptions about the effect of differences in age and sex.

In many intermanagerial negotiations this influence is much more subtle. Indeed, it may not be used consciously by the more senior of the managers involved who may well be unaware that status differences are inhibiting the contribution to a discussion of more junior staff. In a project report submitted for Stage 3 of the Institute of Personnel Management's examination, a junior personnel officer described his experience as a member of an interdepartmental working party which was planning an office reorganization. A situation arose in which he felt the working party made the wrong decision about retraining the office staff. Explaining this, he wrote: 'At about this time I became aware that I was the most junior member of the working party. I think this prevented me from arguing as forcibly as I should have done for more attention to be paid to the staff's retraining needs.'

The message for senior managers is never to underestimate the inhibiting influence perceptions of status may have on more junior staff, including those in other departments than their own. Junior staff need to think through this issue in a positive manner and realize that in specific situations outside the direct executive line, their status derives from their expertise relative to the issue under discussion, and not from their hierarchical position – let alone from differences of salary, age or sex.

Connections with sources of power: Status can, of course be used manipulatively to 'squash' a less senior opponent. One equally manipulative response is for the junior to let it be seen that he or she has 'connections'. Suppose, for example, that the personnel officer in the earlier example had been able to drop into her conversation with the purchasing manager: 'I was having lunch with the Chairman last Sunday and he was asking whether all the heads of departments had been through the equal opportunities training programme.' This should certainly set the alarm bells ringing. Lunch with the Chairman? And on Sunday? Better be careful!

This is again a rather crude example just to highlight the point. Generally, a manager's connections with important power sources do not have to be spelled out. They become known and are then an unspoken influence on intermanagerial negotiations. What they do, in effect, is alter the power balance, and they are therefore of particular value to the manager who is otherwise in a weak bargaining position. In one local authority, the Leisure Centre Manager (a not very highly graded middle managerial post) gained an influence out of all proportion to his formal status because of his skill in exploiting the strong personal enthusiasm of the Leader of the Council for indoor sports. More senior managers became very wary of opposing his ideas or requests in case this was relayed to the Leader. Eventually, however, it became evident that the strength of this connection was far greater in myth than reality. Once this was realized, the manager's general standing fell well below the level which his job otherwise justified, an outcome which illustrates the danger of over-reliance on sources of power other than those which stem directly from legitimate, personal factors.

Nevertheless, in almost all managerial bargaining it is advisable to be aware of informal power groups or circuits. Who has links with whom? From whence might either party summon reinforcements? Assessments of relative strength are necessary if bargaining expectations are to be realistic.

Creating obligations: As with industrial relations, negotiation between managers takes place between parties whose relationship extends beyond the individual bargaining episodes. The psychology of the interaction between two managers who are negotiating is therefore strongly influenced by the much wider general quality of their whole working relationship. At its simplest, if this relationship is friendly, constructive, and is based on mutual respect, then their bargaining episodes are likely to be equally soundly based, with outcomes derived far more from a rational analysis of the issues than from point-scoring, face-saving or considerations of status or influence.

The converse is that a working relationship tainted by personal animosity or fear will lead to any bargaining episode being treated as a conflict in which winning or losing will take precedence over producing solutions.

Some managers, aware of the strength of such influences, set out quite deliberately to create a sense of obligation among their colleagues. They will be ultra-helpful on issues which are not of major concern to them in order to build up a stock of good-will to be called on when their turn comes to want something from other managers. So the purchasing manager's phone may ring. It is the devious production controller calling: 'Hallo George! Jim here. I've just heard from Pauline that your secretary has gone down with flu and Personnel can't find a replacement until next week. As it happens my office is a wee bit slack at the moment and my secretary would be very willing to come over for a couple of days and give you a hand. Are you interested?'

George accepts the offer gratefully. A month later he runs into Jim in the staff canteen and they have lunch together. They talk rugby. 'Didn't know you were such a fan', says Jim. (Actually, he did!) 'I think I could get you a couple of tickets for the Wales/Ireland match if you're interested.' And again, George accepts the offer. A few weeks later, another phone call: 'Hallo George! Jim here. Can I come across and have a chat about getting some decent furniture for my office? I know it's not in the official replacement schedule this year, but you've seen how grotty it is and I'm sure you know how to bend the rules just this once!' To which George's reply should be that the whole point of the schedule is to deal with this particular matter fairly between all the managers. But will he feel able to set aside the sense of obligation which Jim has created by his friendly previous favours?

The wise manager, while firmly determined to develop constructive working relationships in a general sense, will be very wary of accepting unsolicited gifts (actual or metaphoric), however innocent such offers may appear. If the creation of a sense of obligation is a powerful bargaining tool, the only effective counter is to avoid obligations being created.

The power of knowledge: Earlier in this chapter it was said that within the context of a bargaining episode, a manager's legitimate power or strength derives from his or her expertise in the issue under debate. This is indeed the major counter to the negative and manipulative influences with which the previous sections have been mainly concerned. In the short term, young, junior managers may find their negotiating position undermined by the wiles of older, more senior and cynical managers who are more skilled in the craft of organizational politics. In the longer term, they will succeed in influencing the outcome of intermanagerial discussions primarily by demonstrating that they know their subject matter and can produce good ideas.

But the mere possession of knowledge and ideas is not enough. The manager has to project these into the discussion in a way which makes an impact both on the outcome, and on his or her reputation. To rely solely on verbal interjections may not be enough, particularly for the less experienced manager who may feel inhibited by status differences.

One effective way of gaining attention and of concentrating a discussion on a particular issue is to distribute a document which highlights the point concerned. This might be in the form of a chart or graph, or a statistical table, or a list of key features. It needs to be simple or it will be set aside. It needs to be well-prepared – no smudgy photocopies. It can be introduced once it has become evident that no easy agreement is being reached, and preferably at a point in the discussion when some frustration at lack of progress is beginning to be felt. Its impact can be illustrated by an example.

A shoe manufacturing company was experiencing a wave of customer complaints about the soles coming unstuck on a new style. A meeting was held to discuss the problem. Four managers attended – two production superintendents, the materials controller and a laboratory supervisor. Each of the production superintendents had a firmly held theory about the cause of the problem, supported by at least some practical evidence which seemed to indicate faults in the new sole material. The materials controller disputed this, and quoted other evidence which pointed to shortcomings in production methods. The laboratory supervisor, the most junior of the four, attempted to explain some rather complex scientific and statistical analysis which led in a different direction, but through inexperience and some lack of assertiveness, failed to gain attention. Until, that is, she said: 'It might be helpful to look at this chart', and handed round copies of a diagram in colour which showed in graphic form that the probable cause was the use of one particular adhesive at times when the humidity of the air rose above a certain value. From that point in the discussion, the laboratory supervisor in effect became the discussion leader and it was her suggestions for solving the problem which were soon agreed.

An extension of this approach is the more formal presentation of proposals or analysis by the use of flip charts or wall board. This cannot be done so spontaneously as the tabling of a document in the course of a meeting unless, as in IBM, flip chart presentations are accepted as a normal practice in management meetings. When they can be arranged, they can determine the whole structure of a meeting and they therefore give the presenter a degree of influence which may be out of all proportion to his or her formal, hierarchical status – provided, of course, that they are well-prepared and demonstrate mastery of the issues with which they deal.

Commercial negotiation

The most common type of commercial negotiation is concerned with buying and selling – whether of goods or services – and with the associated topics of quality, specification, delivery and service. Lying behind all such transactions is the concept of the conclusion of a contract. Bargaining is necessary in order to bring the buyer's needs and what the seller has to offer into coincidence. At that point a deal is struck. One offers, the other accepts, and both then incur obligations to put their deal into effect. If, to secure a deal, either has made promises or given assurances which in the outcome cannot be met, the other will have access to remedies to nullify the deal and to recompense for any loss which may have been incurred.

The simplicity of the final deal – in essence, a yes to a price – coupled with the need for precision about the parties' intentions which is implied by the concept of a contract, give commercial negotiation a degree of clarity and definition which is often greater than in intermanagerial or industrial relations bargaining. Negotiation is limited to the specifics of the deal which is under consideration. Strategies and tactics can be more precise.

Two other factors lead in the same direction. First, the commercial relationship between a buyer and a seller is, actually or potentially, impermanent and is limited to the trading role. Either party can decide that the other is not able or willing to meet their requirements, and can seek a trading relationship elsewhere. This luxury of choosing an alternative bargaining partner is not open to the industrial relations negotiator or to the manager who has to maintain a working relationship with colleagues despite having at times to play an adversarial role in intermanagerial negotiations.

Second, the balance of power in a buying-selling situation is generally in favour of the buyer. When bargaining with trade unions or trying to influence managerial colleagues, the distribution of power is often much more difficult to assess or predict. It may be argued that there are sellers' as well as buyers' markets: that the advantages in commercial negotiation are not all one way. Of course, situations do arise in which a supplier corners a market, or in which a buyer has some crisis requirement for goods or services which only one seller can provide within the needed time-scale. Generally, though, it is the seller who starts with the built-in disadvantage of having to overcome the buyer's resistance, or of knowing that the buyer can turn to alternative sources of supply. Anyone who doubts this should examine the literature on the subject. Literally hundreds of books have been published on the art of salesmanship: but on the art of buying the bibliography is all but non-existent. The same is true in the field of training. Sales training is one of the most extensive and lucrative of training topics for specialist consultancies and course providers. It is extremely rare to see any training programme offered on the subject of buying.

A significant part of sales training is consequently aimed at helping the sales person overcome the very major disadvantage of the buyer's ability simply to say no – and to go elsewhere. Some of the simplistic selling ploys incorporated into many sales training programmes are:

Emphasize the differences between your product or service and its competitors. Avoid direct price competition by projecting your product as unique.

Flatter the buyers as persons of discretion and wisdom who are able quickly to perceive the specific advantages of the product to their particular business and so gain advantage over their competitors.

Encourage the buyers to feel uneasy about not keeping up-to-date with new developments and products. Suggest that their competitors may steal a march on them by getting in first.

Suggest that delay in placing an order may carry the disadvantage of a price rise – or that an immediate order will carry unusually favourable terms.

These are all fairly crude tactics. Put as simply as this they may seem applicable more to the doorstep salesman of double-glazing than to negotiation between the managers of two companies about, say, a major contract for the supply of components, or the repricing of the lease of an office block. Yet many of the standard methods of the successful retail sales person can be identified in the apparently more sophisticated world of corporate commercial bargaining.

Winkler, a marketing expert whose book, *Bargaining for results*, was referred to in Chapter 4, gives 10 tips for bargaining which are not so simplistic as many conventional sales techniques:

1   *Don't bargain if you don't have to.* This is a good general tip in most negotiations. Why get into a situation in which you may

have to make concessions if you can get what you want without opening the bargaining door.

2   *Be prepared.* Another general point – the need to research the other party's position, to test your own, and consider objectives and tactics.

3   *Let the other side do the work.* Winkler suggests making an important or major demand in the opening stage, so forcing the other party to take on the hard task of trying to obtain concessions.

4   *Apply your power gently at first.* This may seem to conflict with the previous tip, but is a somewhat different point. The idea is to reveal the strength of one's own position gradually – not to show one's whole hand at the beginning.

5   *Make the other party compete.* This tip is of particular relevance to commercial negotiation. It suggests letting the other party think that you have alternative suppliers or customers in mind, so that they feel in competition and at risk of losing out to some third party.

6   *Leave yourself room.* A more general point which applies in all forms of negotiation. This is to ensure that you retain some room for manoeuvre, normally by asking for more than you would ultimately be prepared to accept, and initially conceding less than you might eventually be willing to accede.

7   *Keep your integrity.* Some of Winkler's tips may imply being devious, cunning and tough. He emphasizes, though, the importance of never lying, and of keeping to any commitment you may make.

8   *Listen, don't talk.* The value of asking questions as a negotiating ploy has been referred to in an earlier chapter. It implies, as Winkler suggests, that the less you talk and the more you listen, the more you will learn about the other side's case, and the less they will learn about yours.

9   *Keep in contact with their hopes.* This tip is concerned with the avoidance of breakdown. Push the other party too far or too fast and you may break the negotiating relationship.

10 *Let them get used to your big ideas.* This is a related point. Given that you have stated your top line at an early stage, be patient in dealing with the other side's responses, don't try to rush a settlement, allow time for them to adjust to the level at which you have pitched your position.

Some types of commercial negotiation are undertaken by lawyers acting for their company clients. This is frequently the case where complex business contracts are being prepared, or when a dispute exists which might otherwise lie to be detected in the courts. This form of negotiation imposes some restrictions on the direct participants' bargaining freedom, but also provides opportunities to control the pace of negotiations and to eliminate unwanted personal or emotional influences.

A lawyer acting as a representative will normally have specific limits placed on his or her authority to make bargaining concessions and may frequently have to refer back to the client for further instructions. This provides scope for introducing delays should a long time-scale be to the advantage of one or other party. It is a role, however, which allows a good deal of flexibility to the two negotiators in exploring possible settlements without commitment. 'Might your client consider this, if my client were to offer that?' This is the sort of sounding process which lawyers can adopt without anyone losing face and without the risk of having been thought to offer firm concessions. In one sense, two lawyers negotiating on behalf of their clients can play almost a dual conciliation role in considering possibilities which the clients themselves have either not thought of or might feel inhibited in suggesting.

Lord Goodman, a lawyer of international renown, once said that the most important attribute of an effective negotiator was the determination to reach an agreement. This is of particular importance when two negotiators meet who are of equal competence in the various ploys and skills described in this book. It might be thought that this would inevitably result in deadlock. That would occur, though, only if each had the objective of refusing to be beaten by the other. But if negotiators keep in mind that their goal is an acceptable agreement, not a personal victory, stalemate will not occur. If it did, both negotiators would feel a sense of failure.

Negotiating effectively

There are lessons here for all forms of negotiation. Consider the equivalent in an industrial relations context of the commercial negotiator's emphasis on business objectives. How often in wage bargaining are detailed analyses and projections produced of such matters as the distribution of earnings between basic pay, overtime and bonus, or of the numbers and costs of employees on different points of their salary scales? How often are concessions made without time out being taken to calculate their full effect on direct and indirect costs? How often is the final package vetted not just for cost but for compatibility with the organization's more general business policies or style?

Industrial relations practitioners could learn much from their business colleagues about the need, and the methods used, to ensure that the parameters and outcome of negotiation are kept within acceptable business limits.

Effective negotiation is more than just securing a settlement as near as possible to one's opening position. It also implies ensuring that the settlement is consistent with, and contributes to the achievement of, the organization's whole business objectives and purpose. Winning in the narrow sense of scoring points off the opposition can all too easily become an end in itself. Effective commercial negotiators dealing, for example, with establishing a sound supply contract, realize that merely to exploit superior buying power may achieve an immediate low price contract – but at the cost of destroying the supplier's ability to sustain a reasonably profitable and therefore reliable long term service. Similar considerations about the long term effect of wage settlements on employee motivation or on an organization's ability to recruit satisfactorily, should influence the effective industrial relations negotiator. Effective negotiation is rarely limited to the sheer exploitation of a power advantage. The best settlement is one in which both sides can recognize their own and mutual advantages.

Bibliography

ACAS. *An industrial relations handbook.* London, HMSO. 1980.
ACAS. *Code of practice: Disclosure of information to trade unions for collective bargaining.* London, ACAS. 1976.
ATKINSON G C. *The effective negotiator.* London, Quest. 1975.
BACK K. & K. *Assertiveness at work.* Maidenhead, McGraw-Hill. 1982.
COKER E. *Trade union negotiations.* London, Arrow. 1976.
FISHER R. and URY W. *Getting to yes: Negotiating agreement without giving in.* London. Hutchinson. 1983.
IDS. *Disclosing bargaining information. IDS brief.* London, Incomes Data Services. 1979.
KENNEDY G. *Everything is negotiable.* London, Business Books. 1983.
KENNEDY G. BENSON J. and MACMILLAN J. *Managing negotiations.* London, Business Books. 1980.
KNIVETON B. and TOWERS B. *Training for negotiations.* London, Business Books. 1978.
MARCHINGTON M. *Managing industrial relations.* London, McGraw-Hill. 1982.
MUIR J. *Industrial relations procedures and agreements.* London, Gower. 1981.
STUBBS D. *How to use assertiveness at work.* Aldershot, Gower. 1986.
THOMASON G. *A textbook of industrial relations management.* London, Institute of Personnel Management. 1984.
WALTON R E. and McKERSIE B. *A behavioural theory of labour negotiations.* New York, McGraw-Hill. 1965.
WARR P. *Psychology and collective bargaining.* London, Hutchinson. 1973.
WINKER J. *Bargaining for results.* London, Heinemann. 1981.